A CHANGING AMERICA

A CHANGING AMERICA

SEEN THROUGH ONE SHERWOOD FAMILY LINE 1634–2006

VOLUME TWO

Generations 9 and 10

Frank P. and Frances H. Sherwood

iUniverse, Inc.
New York Lincoln Shanghai

A CHANGING AMERICA
SEEN THROUGH ONE SHERWOOD FAMILY LINE 1634–2006

Copyright © 2006 by Frank P Sherwood

All rights reserved. No part of this book may be used or reproduced by any means, graphic, electronic, or mechanical, including photocopying, recording, taping or by any information storage retrieval system without the written permission of the publisher except in the case of brief quotations embodied in critical articles and reviews.

iUniverse books may be ordered through booksellers or by contacting:

iUniverse
2021 Pine Lake Road, Suite 100
Lincoln, NE 68512
www.iuniverse.com
1-800-Authors (1-800-288-4677)

ISBN-13: 978-0-595-39962-8 (pbk)
ISBN-13: 978-0-595-67765-8 (cloth)
ISBN-13: 978-0-595-84350-3 (ebk)
ISBN-10: 0-595-39962-2 (pbk)
ISBN-10: 0-595-67765-7 (cloth)
ISBN-10: 0-595-84350-6 (ebk)

Printed in the United States of America

CONTENTS VOLUME 2

Chapter I 1
   Clarence[9] MacKinlay Sherwood: His Development and Career 1
   Education 2
       Albany High School 2
       Wesleyan University 3
       Teaching Interlude in Hackensack, N.J. 5
       Doctoral Work at Cornell University 5
   Early Positions 8
       Cincinnati 8
       Philadelphia 8
   Affiliation with Hercules Powder Company 9
       The San Diego Opportunity 9
       The Significance of Potash and Getting It from Kelp 10
       Factories Emerge: The Hercules Plant in San Diego 14
       Move to Wilmington, Delaware 17
       Transfer to Brunswick 18
   Clarence[9] Sherwood Dies March 5, 1923 20

Chapter II 23
   Clarence[9] MacKinlay Sherwood and Mildred Kirk Persons:
   The Linkage of Families; the Birth of an Heir; Death 23
   Mildred Kirk Persons and Her Family Antecedents 24
       John Pearson of Yorkshire 24
       Edward Nathan Persons 26
   Mildred's Parents: Joseph Kirk Persons and Elizabeth (Bess) James 27
       The James Family and Settlement in Red Jacket 27
       Kirk Sets Up in Duluth, Minnesota and Begins His Family 28
   The Family Moves and the Adventures Begin 30

    The James Family Settles on San Diego, California 30
    The Keeley Cure Disaster 31
    The 25th Street House 32
    The Persons Family in Salt Lake City, Utah 33
Everyone in San Diego 34
    Silver Mining in Ensenada, Mexico 35
    The Ensenada Fiasco and Its Consequences 36
    Salome Dies and the Family Power Structure Changes 37
    Ocean Beach Property 38
    The Decline of Ocean Beach 39
Big Changes in Mildred's Life: Becoming an RN and Marriage 40
    In Training at Agnew Hospital 40
    Mildred Named Head of the Infirmary at Hercules Potash Plant;
    Romance with Clarence[9] MacKinlay Begins 41
    Brief Time in Wilmington, Delaware 43
    And Then the Move to Brunswick, Georgia 43
The Death of Clarence[9] 44
    Family Finances 45
    Back to San Diego 46
    On Their Own About Two Years 47
Deaths in the Family 48
    Kirk was First 48
    And It Required Bess to Learn to Drive at Age 60 48
    Joseph Henry James Was the Second to Go 49
    His Father Followed Him Two Years Later 49
    Bess, the Matriarch, Dies in 1943 50
The Great Influence of Both Mother and Grandmother on Frank[10] 51
    Vignettes about Bess and Her Specialness 51
    Mildred: the Central Figure in Frank's Early Life 53
Mildred Persons Sherwood Dies on November 19, 1978 55

Chapter III 56
  Frank[10] Persons Sherwood, the Tenth Generation 56
  Early Memories of Frank[10] Persons Sherwood 56
    Brooklyn Elementary School 57
    Golden Hill Playground 58

Roosevelt Junior High School *59*
    Growing Friendship with Eddie Self *60*
    Wilbur Folsom and First Tennis *60*
    Two Special Teachers *61*
San Diego High School *61*
    Outstanding Faculty *62*
    The Russ School Newspaper: Consuming Interest and Superb
    Development Vehicle *62*
    Tom Ludwig Makes the Ed and Frank[10] Relationship
    a Triumverate *63*
    Grade Success *64*
Time off from School: The Trip East and Working at
The San Diego Sun *65*
    Trip to New York and Washington, D.C. *66*
    Classified Advertising Salesman *66*
    Planning for College *67*
Dartmouth College *67*
    Frank Joins Ed Self at Dartmouth *68*
    Class of 1926 Fellowship *69*
Three Years of Service in the U.S. Army *70*
Operating a Small Newspaper with Ed Self *72*
Marriage! *76*

Chapter IV **80**
    Frances Howell, Wife of Frank[10] Persons Sherwood, Tenth Generation *80*
    The Robinson Family *82*
    Verna Goes to California with Frances *85*
    John Virgil and the Howell Family *90*
    Frances' First Ten Years *91*
    San Diego: A New Life with Fred Tyler *93*
        The Restaurant on University Avenue *95*
        Roosevelt Junior High School *95*
    The High School Years, 1941-1944, within a Context of War *96*
    On to College in the Fall, 1944 ....*98*

Chapter V **101**
  *Frank[10] Persons Sherwood and Frances Howell: The Linkage of Two Families
  and the Birth of Two Children* *101*
  Momentous Events: The Sale of the North Shores Sentinel *102*
  Momentous Events: The New Enterprises and a Disastrous Fire *104*
  The Move to Los Angeles *110*
  Vignettes That Cover 20 Years of Family Life *112*
    Pre-school years *112*
    Pre-High School Years *114*
    Virginia- High School and College *117*
    College (1972-76) *118*
  *A More Systematic Summary of Sherwood Family
  Events During 1953-1976* *119*
  The 10th Generation of Sherwoods from 1977 to 2006 (The Present) *123*

Appendix One 127
Appendix Two 141
Index, Volume 2 173

CHAPTER I

Clarence[9] MacKinlay Sherwood: His Development and Career

As is undoubtedly apparent from the last chapter, there was a great tragedy in the life of Clarence[9] MacKinlay Sherwood. He died far too young. His parents suffered greatly from the loss, but it was Clarence[9] whose future was ended.

This chapter will reveal a young man of tremendous capability, high spirits and enthusiasm, with the capacity to give and receive love, and who had accomplished a great deal in a very short time. It would be wonderful to know how his life might have developed over a more normal span of time.

Aside from his family, a person who deeply appreciated Clarence[9] was Frank Carruth. The two were boyhood friends when Frank[8] Sherwood was the Methodist minister in the town of Cohoes, N.Y. for three years. It was in this period that Clarence[9] and Frank developed a lifetime friendship, which is to be seen in their spending four years together at Wesleyan and then graduate work in Chemistry at Cornell University. How profound was that relationship is expressed in the obituary Frank wrote for the *Cornell Chemist*.[1] His love and respect for Clarence[9] comes through in a truly beautiful testimony to his dear friend. Carruth's feelings and also his data about aspects of the life of Clarence[9] have been invaluable in preparing this chapter.[2]

Clarence[9] operated with several names. These were not aliases but nicknames, and it does cause some difficulty in identifying the best way in which to refer to him. There is a desire to use a more intimate name just because a son writing

---

[1] F.E. Carruth, "Clarence McKinlay Sherwood, A.B., PhD., *Cornell Chemist*, 12:47. (There is no date given, but it likely was 1923.)

[2] In his letters home to his mother Frank[10] wrote about the one meeting he had with Frank Carruth and his family. It occurred in early September, 1942. He wrote: "….I headed for Hackensack, New Jersey, and spent the night with Frank Carruth. He is a wonderful guy, Mom. I liked him an awful lot, so natural and good fun. He has two daughters and a son. One daughter is married, the other was at home and quite nice looking, 19 years old. The son, whose name is also Frank, is in Air Corps Communications."

about his father feels that way. Clarence[9] was known in the family as Clare, in college according to the yearbook as Cance [uncomfortably close to the disease that took his life], to his wife and friends in Brunswick as Doc, and in his financial records as C.M. Yet these various possibilities do not lend themselves easily to the purposes of this chapter. It seems best to stick with the formal name. He will be Clarence[9].

Education

Albany High School

Before arriving at Albany High School in 1901 Clarence[9] had received his education in six different cities in eight years. It must have been quite a treat to be fixed in one place for the whole of the high school period. Most certainly he did very well academically. We have two certificates from the Regents of the University of New York, the first awarded at the end of the freshman year and the other at the conclusion of the senior. In the first, awarded June, 1902, he was recognized as having completed all the required courses in reading, writing, spelling, elementary English, arithmetic, and geography. In addition he was cited for having successfully negotiated examinations in four special subjects: first year Latin, algebra, civics, and drawing.

In January, 1905, the Regents awarded him an Advanced Academic Diploma "certifying to the completion of the fifth academic or thirteenth school year.". The system operated on a "12 count" basis, the credit given for having passed a full year of academic courses. Clarence[9]'s special diploma certified that he was a "60-count" man. On the diploma, too, was a list of 22 courses he had passed that appeared to lie beyond the normal curriculum. They were: Advanced English,

---

"We sat around and he showed me some old Wesleyan stuff, and we talked a good deal about Wesleyan and Dartmouth and compared notes in general. He said that he was the main reason my father did not get into Phi Beta Kappa, and I could understand why. The guy never went to class. He had a whole stack of cards, which had been sent to him for cutting more classes than the limit. He kept the darndest things, for instance records of all his failures, etc.

"Mr. Carruth is still with the Maywood Chemical Co. and seems to have a pretty good job. They have lived in the same house for 25 years, but all the kids are getting good educations and they seem to live pretty nicely. Mrs. Carruth was a swell person, too. I had an awful lot of fun, and they have asked me to come again, which I am going to do." *(September 14, 1942)*

English composition, Latin 1st and 2nd years, Cicero's Orations, Virgil's Aeneid, Latin Prose composition, Xenophon's Anabasis, Homer's Iliad, Algebra, Advanced Algebra, Plane Geometry, Solid Geometry, Physical Geography, Zoology, Physiology and Hygiene, Greek history, Roman history, English history, Elementary U.S. history, Civics, Drawing.

Frank Carruth has observed that Clarence[9] was "…equally at home" in athletics. He reported that Clarence[9] led a "strenuous physical life" and was captain of his high school basketball team. Basketball players were not gargantuan in those days, but Clarence[9] was small. He must have been quick and deceptive on the court. Though Carruth does not mention it, it is probable that Clarence[9] was also involved in high school track and tennis. His career at Wesleyan suggests that he got an early start in these sports.

Wesleyan University

Picture of Clarence9 in 1910 *Olla Podrida*

Clarence[9] graduated from high school not long after his 17th birthday and was enrolled at Wesleyan University in Middletown, Connecticut, well before his 18th. The year was 1905.

As we studied his college annual, the *Olla Podrida,* there were two rather strange features. The first is that the 1909 yearbook carries a date of 1910. Our earlier, rather casual perusal of the book led us to believe that Clarence[9] was the Class of 1910. Close examination revealed, however, that the featured people, i.e. those with individual pictures and clearly graduates, were members of the class of 1909. An earlier *Olla Podrida* (1909) handled things in the same way. The conclusion: Wesleyan's 1909 class senior pictures are to be found in the yearbook of 1910.

There is further confusion. It appears that the 1910 *Olla Podrida* was published at the very beginning of the 1909 academic year, in September. There is absolutely nothing in the book about events and accomplishments in Clarence[9]'s senior year. The reports of the various athletic teams all dealt with the 1908 season. And the commencement program reported is for June, 1908. To get a full picture of Clarence[9] and his achievements in his senior year, we would need access to the 1911 *Olla Podrida*, strange as that may seem. As a result, we do not have any information on what must have been the most important year in his college life

4   A CHANGING AMERICA

Clarence[9] was not a member of a fraternity at Wesleyan, though these organizations appeared to be very strong at the time. He later told Mildred that he was too poor to afford such a luxury. Instead, he and Frank Carruth were members of the Commons Club, which is given roughly the same presence in the *Olla Podrida*, appearing behind the fraternities. The Commons Club was founded at Wesleyan in 1899 and was apparently the first of its kind. A confederation of such clubs was organized in 1906 and included other institutions: Brown, Middlebury, Norwich, and Union.

One of many problems with the arrangement of the *1910 Olla Podrida* is that there is no information about senior academic honors. Only because we have his Wesleyan diploma do we know that Clarence[9] graduated Cum Laude.

It is apparent that the thrust of Clarence[9]'s academic energies was toward the sciences. Frank Carruth has written, "A chemical 'urge' which pervaded the university at the time won out over the classics and claimed him for Chemistry as a major subject."[3] The Carruth view about the orientation of the college is supported by an analysis of the academic fields of the 29 people then listed as on the faculty in the 1910 *Olla Podrida*. About 40% of the faculty (11) had fields in science and mathematics. The other major area of faculty concentration was language, with 11 members in English, Latin, Greek, and German. The remaining seven faculty members had fields of philosophy, the Bible, history, geography, public speaking, psychology, and economics.

A picture of the Wesleyan facutly in the 1910 *Olla Podrida*

We also have a 1906-1907 *Student Handbook* (his sophomore year), which shows that he attended chapel with great regularity and took the following classes over the two semesters: Physics, Economics, Math II, English Literature, French, Physics, Physiology, Biology II, Logic, Chemistry II. While he undoubtedly fulfilled all the requirements of his major, it is obvious from his sophomore academic schedule that he was receiving a broad liberal arts education.

The individual data provided for Clarence[9] in the yearbook (not including anything for his senior year) was: Class tennis champion (1)[4], class track team

---

[3] Ibid.

[4] The numerals in parentheses refer to the class year in which he was involved. (1) refers, for example, to the freshman year.

(1,2,3), Secretary-Treasurer, Tennis Association (3); President, Tennis Association (4), Varsity track team (3), class basketball team (2), Washington's birthday banquet committee. There was no mention that he was a member of the Mathematical Club, whose roster was listed separately in the Yearbook.

Frank Carruth reports that Clarence[9] was a member of varsity track, tennis, and hockey teams. We assume this is true, but the 1910 annual shows him only on the varsity track team. That would have been in his junior year. Clarence[9] was an outstanding hurdler on the track team. There were two meets, one with Trinity and the other with Amherst, both in May, 1908. In the Trinity meet he was third in the 120 yard high hurdles and in the 220 yard low hurdles. Against Amherst he won the high hurdles and placed second in the low.

Picture of tennis team in 1910 *Olla Podrida.* Clarence[9] is in suit at left.

Tennis appears to have been a real love. For the 1908 season he was the President of the tournament. In that event, three of his four matches were three-set affairs; and he came from behind to win in two of them. The year 1908 was a great one for Wesleyan tennis when the team of Holton and White won the national intercollegiate doubles championship at Longwood, Massachusetts. That was well beyond the normal accomplishment in Wesleyan sports.

Frank Carruth describes Clarence[9] as a "brilliant student," and there can be no doubt that Wesleyan prepared him well for his later doctoral studies at Cornell University.

Teaching Interlude in Hackensack, N.J.

After graduating from Wesleyan in June, 1909, Clarence[9] assumed a position as a teacher of chemistry and other sciences in Hackensack High School, Hackensack, New Jersey. We know nothing about this year in his life, which was likely a waiting period until he could begin his doctoral studies.

Doctoral Work at Cornell University

In the fall of 1910, he moved to Cornell University, in Ithaca, New York, as an assistant in the Department of Chemistry. There he established a relationship with Professor E.M. Chamot and ultimately did his thesis work under him in

Sanitary Chemistry and Bacteriology. He also worked with Professor Chamot in Chemical Microscopy. Carruth reports that Clarence's "minor subjects" were in Agricultural Chemistry under Professor Cavanaugh and in Analytical Chemistry under Professor Lundell. "The greater part of his research was a series of studies on the culture media employed for the bacteriological examination of water."[5]

Chamot and Clarence[9] collaborated on a series of studies that yielded the data for his doctoral research. There was a total of four articles published in the *Journal of the American Chemical Society* that reported the findings of these efforts. How close the collaboration was is seen in the fact that a document entitled "A Study of Stokes Neutral Red Reaction as Applied to the Sanitary Examination of Water," and seeming to be a summary of the dissertation, really contains the last article by Chamot and Sherwood.[6] There is a statement inside the cover that the article contains all the experimental work on the neutral red reaction, which apparently constituted one part of the dissertation. It continues: "That part of the work devoted to the general problem of gas production by bacteria has been omitted. The thesis itself is on file in the Library of Cornell University."

We do not have an off-print of the first article in the series of four, dealing with the bacteriological examination of water. It was published in 1915 in the *Journal of the American Chemical Society*, in vol. 37, on pages 1606-30. The other three are:

"Studies on Culture Media Employed for the Bacteriological Examination of Water: II. Lactose-Peptone Media," *Journal of the American Chemical Society*, 37:1949-59 (August, 1915)

"Studies on Culture Media Employed for the Bacteriological Examination of Water: The Composition of the Gases formed in Lactose-Peptone Fermentation Tubes," *Journal of the American Chemical Society*, 37:2198-2204 (September 1915). (R.C. Lowry is also listed as a co-author on this article.)

"Studies on Culture Media Employed for the Bacteriological Examination of Water:IV. Neutral Red Lactose Peptone Media," *Journal of the American Chemical Society*, 39:1755-1766 (August 1917).

Only chemists would be interested in the details of these studies, which are empirical in character. The methodology was classically experimental.

The work was designed to meet a critical need in the modern society: clean water. Clearly, there is (and was) an imperative for an easy, fail-safe way to ascer-

---

[5] Carruth, *loc. cit.*

[6] E.M. Chamot and C.M. Sherwood, "Studies on the Culture Media Employed in the Bacteriological Examination of Water," *Journal of the American Chemical Society*, 29:1855-66 (August, 1917).

tain water quality. In the early part of the 20th century, the great preoccupation was with the existence of fecal matter. "Since the most important of the fermentative bacteria, from the viewpoint of the water analyst, are those in the *B. coli* group derived from the feces of man and animals, our studies were confined to this group."[7]

The major contribution appears to have been the proposal of a new medium for testing the quality of water. A neutral red complex of peptone, potassium chloride, and lactose was offered as a "very sensitive and accurate medium for the speedy detection of fecal pollution. In fact, it is our belief that the medium is much more sensitive than the standard lactose-bile medium [which apparently had been the common testing solution]."[8]

The quest for the doctorate was not, however, without its problems. The Cornell chemistry laboratory burned down, and all Clarence[9]'s data in it were lost. Those who have studied for a PhD will understand this situation because virtually all candidates have continuing nightmares that their data will be somehow destroyed. In this case the loss was irreparable. It became impossible to support conclusions that had been reached after much fact-gathering and analysis. In a note that appears at the end of an article on his dissertation, Clarence[9] writes:

> It is unfortunate that, owing to the loss of a large amount of data in the burning of the Cornell University chemical laboratory, we cannot give a summary of the results obtained on a very large number of samples covering a period of five years. It is on a careful study of these that we have based our third conclusion. Nor are we able to give the data obtained with 'synthetic media' bearing on our conclusions under II. This paper is presented in its unfinished condition since it would require several years more of work to again obtain data.[9]

---

[7] *Journal of the American Chemical Society, op. cit.,* 37: 1950
[8] *Journal of the American Chemical Society, op. cit.,* 39:1765
[9] Clarence McKinlay Sherwood, "A Study of Stokes Neutral Red Reaction as Applied to the Sanitary Examination of Water," *Journal of the American Chemical Society* 39:1766 (August, 1917)

Early Positions

Cincinnati

Clarence[9] had finished his PhD studies in 1914 and was ready to move on. The pattern is typical for doctoral students. The review and defense of the dissertation take a considerable amount of time. When the process is not completed by June of a given year, the degree will not be awarded until the following June. Someone who successfully defends the dissertation in September, for example, will have no more business at the university but will have to wait about nine months for the award of the degree.

It is not surprising, then, that Clarence[9] became a chemist with the U.S. Public Health Service in Cincinnati. He was certainly there by September, 1914. We can be certain of the date because he went to the national clay court tennis championships in Cincinnati in that month. He took pictures of the title matches and labeled them September, 1914. It is probable that Clarence[9] continued to work on water quality problems because he took pictures of various elements of the Cincinnati water operation.

Philadelphia

With his degree in hand, Clarence[9] was ready for new opportunities. Later in 1915 we find he is the Bacteriologist at the Food Research Laboratory, U.S. Bureau of Chemistry, Department of Agriculture, in Philadelphia. He stayed there until February, 1917, when he was lured to San Diego by the Hercules Powder Co. and left the "purely research life," as Carruth described it.

In Philadelphia Carruth reports that Clarence[9] was involved in the study of the biochemical and bacteriological changes in eggs and chickens in storage. From the standpoint of Professor Chamot, there were two problems with the assignment in Philadelphia: (a) women and (b) chickens and eggs. When Clarence[9] sought his advice on a job in San Diego, Chamot wrote on January 25, 1917, "After smelly eggs and green chickens, rotten kelp ought not to be so bad. It would be a change of smells anyway and you would be your own boss very largely instead of being dominated by a petticoat. [Apparently Clarence[9]'s boss was a woman.] This last feature is one which would influence me most. I've no use for chickens outside their proper sphere. As the Englishman would say—I should think you would be jolly well fed up on eggs."

In reading the Sherwood-Pennington article, one is struck by the ghoulish practices followed in the name of science. Chickens were killed and bled by "sticking through the mouth." "By braining a bird through the eye it frequently turned green in the slaughtering process because of chemical factors. The difficulty was that no one wanted a green chicken, resulting in considerable losses for the industry.[10]

The good news is that Sherwood and Pennington found a way to avoid the greening problem. You starve the chickens for at least 24 hours before killing them, and you keep the carcasses in a room that is chilled to 32 degrees.

Affiliation with Hercules Powder Company

The San Diego Opportunity

Before accepting the offer to join Hercules in San Diego, Clarence[9] sought the advice of his old professor, E.M. Chamot, as previously noted. Aside from his disdain for the work in Philadelphia, Chamot wrote the following about the new job and possibilities:

Hiking trip, possibly when Clarence[9] was in Philadelphia, 1915-17. He is at lower right.

> If you do not object to going to California, I would advise you to take the job—it ought to be a most interesting one, but I anticipate, one which will tax all your knowledge and ingenuity. . That, however, is the interesting and attractive side of the problem. You ask for suggestions: I know nothing of the nature and character of the problems involved. If after you "get on the job" you care to write me for details of just what you are up against I will gladly give you what I have, granting that I have any ideas at all. I imagine (and I guess imagine is the right word) that it will be largely a question of what group of fermenting organisms cause you trouble. Sea water organisms? If so, I don't know a thing about them other than that they are a most amazingly interesting lot. Beijernck was working on them when I was in Delft and he had a number of curious species. If you can find his contributions to the bacterial flora of seawater it might help. Much of this has been published in Dutch in various Journals of the different Netherlands societies. You ought not to find Dutch difficult to translate. Doubtless almost all of it has been abstracted in the Centralblalt fur Bact. u. parasit. I think, too, you will find much of it in Mace's Bacteriologie.[11]

---

[10] C. M. Sherwood and M. E. Pennington, "The Greening of Poultry," *Poultry Science*, 1:114-24 (April-May, no year)

[11] Letter to C.M. Sherwood from E.M. Chamot, dated January 25, 1917

Carruth records a statement by L.N. Bent, whom he identifies as "one of the prominent officials" of Hercules: "Dr. Sherwood was sent immediately to San Diego to assist in the organization and development of a large war plant which was being erected by the Hercules Company to produce acetone, potash, and other organic chemicals for our own and the allied governments."[12]

From Carruth's standpoint, the assignment was a great one for all parties. He wrote: "Dr. Sherwood was exactly the right type of man to successfully prosecute the work in hand. Possessing an exceptionally keen and well-trained mind, he also had the unusual ability of understanding human nature and getting other people to pull together and put forth their best efforts. In other words, he was the rare combination of a real scientist and a good executive."[13]

Clarence[9] began his new job in San Diego in February 1917, soon after the new plant was completed.

It is striking to reflect on the mobility of this young man and what a major change had occurred in little more than a generation. Both his grandfathers were rooted on their farms, one dying in the house in which he was born. Clarence[9]'s father had moved a bit, but not much. Less than 29 years of age, Clarence[9] had gone to college in Connecticut, taught in New Jersey, done his doctoral work in New York, had an assignment in Cincinnati and another in Philadelphia, and in 1917 he was across the country in San Diego. When his short life ended, he would also have spent another year in the Mid-Atlantic (Delaware) and more than two years in the deep south, in Brunswick, Georgia.

The work in San Diego was truly at the frontier. Although seaweed does not seem to possess excitement, the story of the development of the Hercules potash plant ought to occupy at least a small niche in American industrial history. Professor Chamot was certainly right that Clarence[9] was embarked on an enterprise that was both new and uncharted. Because Clarence[9] was so much a part of the effort, it is appropriate to describe the undertaking in substantial detail.[14]

The Significance of Potash and Getting It from Kelp

What was unique about the Hercules plant in San Diego was its seeking to obtain a frequently used material, potash, from a new and unique source, seaweed.

---

[12] Carruth, *loc. cit.*

[13] Ibid.

[14] From a monograph by Frank P. Sherwood, *San Diego's World War I Potash Plant: An Unlikely Site for a Romance.* Tallahassee, Fl.: January, 2000, xeroxed, 7 p.

Potash, which is potassium carbonate, has long been valued because of its potassium content. The first important usage seems to have been as fertilizer. It was well established that wood ashes, which contain potash, function as plant nutrients. Pliny the Elder, writing in the first century AD, counseled the use of wood ashes as a fertilizer. The view that plants need potassium persists to this day, though we do recognize that plants have other requirements as well.

Potash also has an important industrial usage in glass manufacture, dating back before the 17th century. Soft soap is another significant product requiring potash.

The recognition that potassium is an important element in the natural world has emerged only in the last 200 years. In 1807 Sir Humphry Davy connected a piece of solid potash to the poles of a battery and caused the release of a metal at the negative pole. He named the metal potassium and determined many of its physical and chemical properties.

At some point in this long chain of developments, it was discovered that potassium can be an important contributor to the manufacture of explosives. Potassium chlorate is a white crystalline compound and is a powerful oxidizing agent used in matches, fireworks, and explosives. Potassium is far too reactive to exist in a free state and thus is found combined with other minerals. It can be mined and distilled from various compounds.

In the period before World War I, Germany had developed a virtual monopoly on the mining of potash. Its dominance came primarily because of the efficiency of its mines. Potash could be found in many different places, but the problem was to extract it from large masses in low cost ways. Rather than develop new mines and face the problem of competing with German efficiency, users in the United States tended to import the potash they needed.

By 1914 the picture changed dramatically. World War I created a major new imperative, though an article in the *Los Angeles Times* in 1914 indicated that the problem was broader and more pervasive. The *Times* painted a gloomy picture and emphasized how critical potassium was:

> The fact that Germany absolutely controls all the available potash of the world, and the reasonable uncertainty of that supply, caused by the recent flooding and complete ruin of some of their mines, has caused the rest of the world a general, and [in] the United States a particular unrest, for, when Germany consumes the entire output of its mines within its own borders or refuses to export the material, or if the supply should fail through any cause, all vegetable and plant life now used as a food supply would soon be eliminated, and animal life would follow soon. International wars would be a thing of the past, or fought as our forefathers fought them, with stones, clubs, arrows and spears. Our celebrations would certainly be safe and sane, as fireworks and explosives could not be

made. Our fires would be started with the flint and steel as no matches could be manufactured. Without the potassium compounds our physicians' occupation would be lost. Therefore, the magnitude of an enterprise of this scale can hardly be estimated, or can the profits accruing therefrom be computed by any system of figures now at our command.

These conditions have caused a worldwide search for some other potash supply, which has been carried on for over twenty years by the different nations through proper organization effected for that purpose; by capitalists, through their engineers and employees; by scientists and engineers, on their own responsibility, and particularly by the United States government in the interest of our national requirements.

The report of certain competent chemists and engineers that seaweed or kelp was known to contain potassium and other valuable products, and that the Pacific kelps contained three and half times more potassium than kelps of any other region, induced the United States government to make a special research to determine its full extent and value in order to classify it as a national asset, and to encourage the harvesting of kelp to satisfy these national wants.[15]

Thus, one answer to the potash shortage was to get it from seaweed, more specifically kelp. It is a remarkable plant that tends to grow close to shore, not out in the recesses of the ocean. The forests of kelp are huge, rising as much as 10 stories, 150 to 200 feet. A kelp forest is like one on land. And kelp grows fast, one to two feet per day. There is no problem of reforestation. The supply of kelp is virtually infinite.

Early entrepreneurs in California were eying the possibilities of kelp just after the turn of the century. Certainly one of the earliest to look at kelp seriously was a San Diegan, David M. Balch, who began his inquiries in 1902. He was identified in the *San Diego Union* as the "father of kelp." It was a strange appellation. Certainly he did not invent kelp. In an article written for the *Union*, he recounted his early effort:

> In the winter of 1902 I noticed that masses of giant kelp, lying above the surf line on the Coronado strand, were covered with a heavy unusual appearance in air-dried salts. The unusual appearance of the deposit arrested my attention to the extent that I collected specimens for future study. Analyses in my private laboratory led to the unexpected, in fact amazing, result that the said salts were potassium chloride, almost chemically pure.

---

[15] *Los Angeles Times*, January 1, 1914

> Immediately I began a study of the giant algae of the Pacific coast, and of processes for the advantageous exploitation of the kelp beds, having in the view their utilization as raw material for the commercial production of potash.[16]

He continued his work during the next several years, securing his first patent for extracting potash in 1903 and publishing an article in a scientific journal. In the following years he wrote that it was "pretty well established that the Pacific giant algae were in a class by themselves as most liberal potash containers in comparison with algae from other localities and that they were growing in sufficient abundance to be relied on as steady furnishers of raw material..."[17]

During this period he associated with a man, who lived in Coronado, California (across the bay from San Diego), to interest major manufacturers of chemical products in the undertaking. But they were unsuccessful because the Germans were meeting market needs at relatively low costs. Balch observed that many of the firms were bound to the Germans with long-term contracts, and he found others doubted that potash from kelp could compete economically.

About 1909 Balch gave up on interesting the private sector in the project and turned to the government. He penned letters to members of the executive branch telling them of his work and its promise. Washington listened to the San Diegan and in 1911 ordered an investigation of the possibilities. Surveys of the kelp beds and their prospects were undertaken by the Department of Agriculture in 1911 and 1912. The findings were extremely positive and supported those of Balch, according to W.C. Crandall, who made the studies and wrote an article on them for the same edition of the *San Diego Union* in which Balch's article appeared.[18]

A portion of the Department of Agriculture report was included in a *Los Angeles Times* article, "....In the giant kelp beds of the Pacific Coast there is a potential source of potash salts which can certainly yield annually some three or four times the amounts now used in this country, and under the best management might even rival the famous Strassfurt deposits. It is regarded as a very conservative estimate to put the annual yield of potassium chloride from the Pacific kelps at upwards of 1,000,000 tons, worth at present prices nearly $40,000,000."[19]

---

[16] David M. Balch, *San Diego Union,* January 1, 1917
[17] Ibid.
[18] W.C. Crandall, *San Diego Union,* January 1, 1917
[19] *Los Angeles Times,* January 1, 1914

The *Times* reported that there were others besides Balch interested in kelp. The Coronado Chemical Company was organized in 1908 by Henry S. Firman of San Diego, primarily to exploit kelp for fertilizers. The *Times* did not mention Balch and declared that Firman, along with H. Wilson of San Francisco, held the basic patents for extracting potassium. The *Times* observed that Firman's "latest invention, that of potash extraction from seaweed, is one of the most valuable inventions and chemical discoveries of the age." The firms organized by Firman and Wilson merged as American Potash, and were reported by the *Times* as "….erecting a factory on Long Beach harbor, capable of consuming 2000 tons of green kelp each twenty four hours, producing over 100 tons of potassium salts and by-products of more than equal value."[20]

Factories Emerge: The Hercules Plant in San Diego

W.C. Crandall reports essentially the same pattern of commercial development:

> The first company to enter upon the handling of kelp on a commercial scale was the Coronado Chemical Company at Encinitas. It attempted to produce by a secret process a substance containing soluble potassium salts and phosphates together with certain other substances. Shortly afterward, the Ocean Products Company erected a plant at Half Moon Bay, above Monterey, but these two companies soon united and formed the American Products [Potash] Company with their plant at Long Beach. Thereupon a number of companies sprang up whose main object seemed to be stock selling, and whose principal way of using funds seemed to be overhead expense, with little actual money put into the development of the kelp industry.
>
> The outbreak of the European war, however, turned the attention of large fertilizer and chemical companies to finding in the United States sources for the potash which for many years had been supplied from the Strassfurt mines of Germany, the United States having imported over 900,000 tons of potash salts per year, at a value of over $12,000,000. Investigations were consequently started in many directions, but it was to the kelp of the Pacific Coast that the big companies turned. Swift and Company of Chicago leased the Kelp Products Company's plant at Roseville for a series of experiments, the results of which led to the establishment of a large plant at the foot of G street [in San Diego], with a big battery of driers and a harvester capable of carrying 500 tons of wet kelp.

---

[20] Ibid.

The Hercules Powder Company at about the same time began the establishment of what is now the largest potash plant on the coast...[21]

The move into kelp was so fast and so great that the "father of kelp," David Balch, felt compelled to enunciate words of caution. He wrote, again in 1917, that

...under the stimulus of enormous profits so easily won, the conversion of the Pacific algae into potash is being carried on with feverish energy. In view of permanent injury that may result to this, our most valuable source of an important staple, by the injudicious and unrestrained exploitation of the marine mines that produce it, it is to be hoped that the government may right speedily assume control and that under strict conservation their present value may be permanently assured."[22]

We have no information on why the Hercules Powder Co. decided to invest in a kelp plant in San Diego, particularly one of such major scale. In any case, the project got under way early in 1916. Land was leased from the Santa Fe Railroad, and the *San Diego Union* announced that Hercules would soon begin the construction "of an immense potash plant in the bayfront at Chula Vista."[23] By that time the State Board of Harbor Commissioners had given the company a franchise to construct a 2000 foot wharf for use in connection with a 30 acre chemical plant.

In February 1916 the *San Diego Union* carried the report that Hercules was "rushing work on its new potash plant in Chula Vista," although hampered greatly by flooding. Nearly 100 men were at work on the project, and the number involved was to rise to 1000 as soon as conditions permitted. Approximately 400,000 board feet of redwood lumber, purchased from the McCormick Lumber Co. in San Diego, was being utilized.

"Herbert Talley, representative here of the company," the *Union* reported, "announced yesterday that the plant will be erected and in actual operation in four months if no further delays are encountered..."[24] Apparently the plant construction went on schedule, with operations probably beginning in May or June

---

[21] Crandall, *loc. cit.*
[22] Balch, *loc. cit.*
[23] The newspaper clip carries only a 1916 date but it must have been very early in the year.
[24] *San Diego Union,* February 3, 1916

1916. By mid-July Talley was announcing that the Hercules payroll was nearly $65,000 per month and another $5000 was being spent on supplies. Six hundred people were employed. Further, Hercules was paying wages that were as high as, or higher than, those in any enterprise in the city.

"We have invested $2,000,000 in our plant," Talley said, "and have not yet made a cent of profit." Talley, though, was apparently optimistic about the plant's prospects. He said, "Our company merely secures the raw material at its plant here to be used in the manufacture of gunpowder. We had the courage to make the experiment of extracting potash from kelp; we have succeeded..."[25]

During 1916, the *Union* reported that Hercules and Swift had "mowed" 210,596 tons of seaweed for use in San Diego. About 185,000 of the total came from Hercules ships.

A picture dated 1917 shows 350 people gathered to celebrate the first shipment of 60,000 pounds from the plant. They hold a large sign, saying, "First car- Potash from Kelp 60,000 lbs."

Clearly, things were working. In a very short time, the San Diego operation was making a significant contribution to the war effort.

Even more suddenly than it appeared on the landscape, however, Hercules' potash plant disappeared. The records provide no specific date when it closed, but it must have been very shortly after World War I ended.

When there was a Congressional battle over the taxation of profits triggered by defense spending, the president of the San Diego Chamber of Commerce noted that Hercules had invested $2 millions in the plant "at great experimental risk." And another San Diego businessman, also expressing opposition to the tax, observed that Hercules had made "...an enormous expenditure...in a plant which is more or less experimental in character."

Thus, despite Herbert Talley's proclamation of success for the process of extracting potassium from kelp, it probably came as no surprise that the economic realities of the post-war world did not leave room for kelp as a source of potash.

Again, we rely on Frank Carruth to provide insight on Clarence[9]'s role in the undertaking. He wrote: "At San Diego new processes and products were developed and entirely new methods evolved which made the plant a success and

---

[25] Source for this statement not available.

played a very important part in our government's war program. A very large part of the credit for this belonged to Dr. Sherwood. He was of real service to his country during the war and performed his duty in a manner that should cause his name to be recorded with those of others who took their full burden of responsibility during the world's crisis."[26]

Move to Wilmington, Delaware

By March, 1919, Clarence[9] and his new wife, Mildred, were on their way east to assume a new post at the Hercules Powder Co. Carruth writes that the assignment was with the company's experimental plant at Kenvil, New Jersey. Clarence[9] was engaged in research work, he reported, on various fatty acids and their esters with particular pharmaceutical value. It is likely that the young married couple was living in Wilmington, Delaware, which lay just across the Delaware river from New Jersey. Mildred consistently reported to her son that she and Clarence[9] had lived in Wilmington. If there is a contradiction here, it is impossible to reach any definitive conclusions. Kenvil no longer exists on maps, and so there is no way to establish its proximity to Wilmington.

Clarence[9] in about 1920

With the move east, it was clear that Clarence[9] saw his future with the Hercules Powder Co. What was the enterprise like in those days? It was not an old company. It was a spinoff of fabled munitions maker E.I. Dupont, which was hit by an early anti-trust action and was divided into three parts, one of which was the Hercules Powder Co.

Clarence[9] had a small leather folder in which he kept his company ID. On the inside back cover was a brief statement on the company, its products and its offices. It declared that the company was a manufacturer of "explosives of every kind." Products listed were dynamite, extra dynamite, gelatin dynamite, blasting gelatin, permissible powders, blasting powder, and blasting supplies.

Its main office was in Wilmington, Delaware, with 10 other offices or plants across the country.

---

[26] Carruth, *loc. cit.*

Transfer to Brunswick

The assignment to Brunswick (which was so recent an acquisition that it was not mentioned in the list of Hercules plants and offices) in late 1919 was very likely a choice one for a young man of about 30 years of age.

What Hercules had received from Dupont was essentially the explosives business. As noted above, anything that had to do with guns and their firing was likely in the Hercules orbit. With the end of World War I and an expected period of lessened armament activity, the company undoubtedly cast around for other opportunities where its expertise could be exploited. Hence the purchase of two plants largely producing turpentine in Brunswick, Georgia. The Hercules intent, however, was to move far beyond turpentine. It sought to develop entirely new products that could be created from white pines. That meant chemical know-how was a prime requisite. Making trees into something else basically involved chemistry.

Thus a person who had a PhD in Chemistry was a rare bird for this rapidly transforming enterprise. The fact that Clarence[9] designed and planned his own laboratory on the plant site suggests how important he must have been in the thinking about the future. Clarence[9]'s ID was issued by A.S. Kloss, the works manager, and identified him as Research Chemist.

Frank Carruth sums up the new job:

> In the spring of 1920, the Hercules Company entered into the Naval Stores business in the south, buying two large plants and building a third. This industry depends on the conversion of waste pulp wood and stumps into products such as resin, turpentine, etc. The whole industry was in its infancy and a large amount of research and development was necessary to make the business commercially successful. Here again Dr. Sherwood's particular ability singled him out as the man to carry on this development, and he was put in charge of all the chemical work pertaining to the operation and development of this phase of the company's business.[27]

L.N. Bent, whom Carruth had identified as a "prominent official in the company" and may have been the head of the Brunswick operation, has always been described as a particular friend and supporter. Mildred spoke warmly and fondly of him. He was inevitably "Mr. Bent," which suggests status. There is an inter-office memo, dated Nov. 14, 1919, which indicates Clarence[9] may have been in

---

[27] Ibid.

Brunswick by that time, though Mildred generally described 1919 as a year in Delaware. Another memo, dated June 27, 1920, is addressed to Bent in Brunswick.

The November memo to Clarence[9] came from N.P. Rood, Vice President in Philadelphia, and made reference to a letter from Clarence[9] to Bent, dated November 2, 1919. It provides detail on a number of experiments and other materials. described as "...excerpts from authorities named in your letter..." Rood concludes, "Please be assured that this department will be glad to assist you in any way we can and we hope you will not hesitate to call on us at any time."[28] The excerpts, all but one in German, seem to be concerned with the development of a certain type of acid, something that might have had significance for the development of new wood products in Brunswick.

The second memorandum directly related to Brunswick undertakings. Addressed to Bent, the memo described a process developed in Toledo for washing resin with sulphuric acid to make lighter colored resin.

Natural resin, it appears, was critical to the development of new products. (This was long before the time of synthetics.) It was typically dark in color and was secreted primarily by pines and firs as a result of injury to the bark from wind, fire, lightning, and other causes. While much resin evaporates, the remainder is soft

The laboratory Clarence[9] designed and planned in Brunswick.

and readily soluble. As it ages, it hardens. Amber is regarded as the hardest natural resin. There were many product uses, the most prominent in lacquers and varnishes. But possibilities went well beyond that. Amber was made into jewelry; and theoretically, with the use of various acid washes, the color of hard resin could be sufficiently changed as to make it even more attractive for jewelry.

---

[28] Memorandum to C.M. Sherwood from N.P. Rood, November 2, 1919.

How far these ideas were carried in the little more than two years that Clarence[9] had for the job is not known. But there can be no doubt that his work was regarded as pivotal for the enterprise.

Clarence[9] Sherwood Dies March 5, 1923

Clarence[9]'s work came to an abrupt end when he died, after an illness of only two months, March 5, 1923. The newspaper in Brunswick, Georgia, carried an obituary and a follow-up article. However, we have only the clippings, which do not include the name of the newspaper or the dates of publication of the articles. [They likely appeared on March 6 and 7, 1923.]

<u>Newspaper Article No. 1</u>
C.M. SHERWOOD
    DIED YESTERDAY
    AT CITY HOSPITAL
POPULAR YOUNG CHEMIST SUC-
CUMBS AFTER BRIEF ILLNESS

Clarence McKinley [sic] Sherwood died at the city hospital yesterday afternoon at 1 o'clock, after an illness of ten days.

Although no hopes had been held out by attending physicians for the past few days for Mr. Sherwood's recovery the news of his death came with peculiar sadness to his many friends in Brunswick, among whom he was held in the highest regard and esteem.

"Doc" Sherwood, as he was affectionately known, came to Brunswick in June, 1920, as head chemist for the Hercules Powder Company, having been transferred from Wilmington, Del., where he had held an important position with the Hercules Powder company. Mr. Sherwood and Mrs. Sherwood soon took a prominent place in Brunswick's social circles. He was a genial, affable young man who made friends with all with whom he was thrown in contact.

It was only a few weeks ago that Mr. Sherwood's health began to fail, and on Saturday, March 24th [This date has to be wrong, as Clarence[9] died on March 5. It was probably February 24.], he was carried to the City hospital for treatment. From the first it was disclosed that there was no hope for him and his family and friends were advised accordingly.

Mr. and Mrs. Frank Sherwood, parents of Mr. Sherwood, were summoned from their home in Albany, N.Y., arriving here a short time before he passed away. A sister of Mrs. Sherwood also came from California, reaching Brunswick Saturday night. In the presence of those nearest and dearest to him, the soul of Clarence Sherwood took its flight. At the home, 918 Egmont Street, last night, short services were held, prior to the journey to Albany, N.Y. this morning, where funeral and interment will be held. A large number of sorrowing friends called to pay their last tribute of esteem and love in which the deceased was held.

Mr. Sherwood was 34 years of age and is survived by his wife and little son.

<u>Newspaper Article No. 2</u>
C.M. SHERWOOD'S
   BODY CARRIED
   TO ALBANY. N.Y.
FUNERAL PARTY LEFT YESTERDAY MORNING ON LONG JOURNEY

The body of popular "Doc" Sherwood, accompanied by his grief stricken widow, his little son, and his father and mother, began its long journey to Albany N.Y., yesterday morning, where all that is mortal of this clever, genial young Brunswickian will be laid to final rest in the family lot in the cemetery in the capital city. [This is incorrect. He was buried in Fort Plain, N.Y.]

The casket was borne to the train from the funeral car by the close personal friends and business associates of the deceased: Messrs. J.P. McLean, C.V. Sitton, A.S. Kloss, Maurice Lockwood, S.H. Tyre, A.A. Shimer, R.K. Cole, and G.A. Perdue. There was a wealth of exquisite floral offerings, tokens of the love and esteem in which Clarence McKinley [sic] Sherwood was held in the hearts of hundreds of friends, who are sorely grieved over his untimely death.

No young man ever came to Brunswick who so readily won a place in the esteem and affection of his fellows as did Mr. Sherwood. Of a genial, happy disposition, he scattered sunshine wherever he was, and his genial companionship was much sought after. He loved his friends, he idolized his wife and baby. His death comes as a staggering blow to them and to his aged parents, all of whom carried with them the sincerest sympathy of many saddened hearts.

Mr. Sherwood was thirty-four years of age, and had held responsible positions with the Hercules Powder Company for several years. He came to Brunswick nearly three years ago from Wilmington, Del. It was only recently that Mr. Sherwood was stricken with what proved to be his fatal illness. Although everything that medical science would suggest was done to alleviate his sufferings, the golden heart of Clarence Sherwood was stilled forever Monday afternoon.

The next chapter will be concerned with Clarence[9]'s marriage, the introduction of the Persons family into the Sherwood line, and the birth of Frank[10].

FAMILY GROUP SHEET

Husband: Clarence MacKinlay Sherwood
Born 01 Apr 1888 in Broadalbin, New York
Married: 25 Dec 1918 San Diego, California
Died: 05 Mar 1923 Brunswick, Georgia
Father Frank Rosevelt Sherwood:
Mother Catherine Anne MacKinlay:

Wife: Mildred Kirk Persons
Born 25 Nov 1895 in Duluth, Minnesota
Died: 18 Nov 1978 Charlottesville, Virginia
Father: Joseph Kirk Persons
Mother: Elizabeth James

CHILDREN
1 Frank Persons Sherwood
Born: 11 Oct 1920 in Brunswick, Georgia
Married: Cleo Frances Howell 14 Feb 1948 in Laguna Beach, California

CHAPTER II

*Clarence[9] MacKinlay Sherwood and Mildred Kirk Persons:
The Linkage of Families; the Birth of an Heir; Death*

> We are at the point where the authors have had personal experiences with many of the key figures. In fact, Frank grew up with most of people whose lives are described in this chapter. That is why the Persons-James family history receives significant attention.
>
> Because there is so much that is personal to be shared, the style of previous chapters that relied heavily on the printed record need no longer be followed. There is now the possibility of a much more personal, anecdotal account of this family.
>
> Because Frank[10] finds it so difficult to separate himself from events and times that he shared, the removed, neutral stance of previous chapters must be amended. From this point on, the perspective is much more that of a participant than of a reporter.

When Clarence[9] arrived in San Diego in early 1917, he very likely had little idea that his life would soon change dramatically. Indeed, it appears that he perceived his time in San Diego as one only in which he had a big professional challenge and responsibility, with the successful conclusion of World War I a prime imperative. It was not a time for socializing. His choice of abode presented something of a signal. He registered at the downtown YMCA and was there until late 1918.

The person who changed things was Mildred Kirk Persons.

And the venue within which the change took place was the Hercules Co. potash plant. It is not often that one conceives of a potash plant as conducive to romance. It was a setting within which about 350 people worked and somewhat surprising that the chemistry between two members of this large group would be such as to spark love.

We do not know exactly how Clarence[9] and Mildred came to know each other at the plant, but they were both in roles that involved engagement with many others in the organization. He was the research chemist and she the head of the infirmary. Another unknown is exactly when she left San Diego's Agnew Hospital to join Hercules. Our guess is, though, that she was employed early in 1918.

In 1918 Mildred was 22 years of age (she became 23 on November 25, just before she got married) and a Registered Nurse. She never said how she got the job at Hercules, but managing an infirmary for 350 employees would seem to be a role of major importance. Holding such a position at an early age is impressive.

Many of the pictures we have suggest that Clarence[9] and Mildred spent considerable time together before their marriage on Christmas day, 1918, at Mildred's parents' house, 759 25th street, in San Diego. They enjoyed a honeymoon at the fabled Mission Inn in Riverside, California. The Inn was in a small desert town east of Los Angeles that had developed a reputation since 1902 as one of the posh hotels in the state. In later years Mildred recalled the honeymoon as one of her fondest memories. Their wedding announcement declared that they would be at home in the Sherman Apartments on 22nd street after January 15, 1919. So it appears they took sufficient time to have a real honeymoon.

Mildred in nurse's uniform at Agnew hospital

Mildred and Clarence[9] standing by the car.

Mildred Kirk Persons and Her Family Antecedents

John Pearson of Yorkshire

Who was Mildred, the person Clarence[9] had brought into the Sherwood line? And what was the character of her family? Before proceeding further with the story of Clarence[9] and Mildred, there is needed reporting on the new family and the genes it brought to the Sherwoods.

The ancestor of the Persons family (John Pearson) arrived in New England just three years after Thomas Sherwood of Fairfield, Clarence[9]'s ancestor, had departed from the ship *Francis* in 1834. So both families shared long histories in the United States and also had a common background in agriculture.[29] We know more about John Pearson's origins in England than we do about those of Thomas, whose roots, as we reported earlier, have been only partially established.

John Pearson was a native of Yorkshire, England, born in 1615. It is interesting that the names Pearce, Pearse, Pierce, Pearson, and Peirson are all thought to have come from the name Peter (Pierre in French). It has been suggested that Pierson is a south-of-England name and Pearson north-of-England. "Pearson is, generally speaking, characteristic of the north of England, and of the midlands, being most frequent in the North and East Ridings of Yorkshire and afterwards in Warwickshire, Northumberland, Cumberland, and Westmoreland."[30]

Thus, John Pearson's birth in Yorkshire seems entirely reasonable. It is also interesting that reported research reveals that the name Pearson appeared 60 times among 10,000 names in the Yorkshire area. On the other hand, the names Pierson and Peirson were rare.[31]

After his arrival in 1637, John Pearson settled in Lynn, Massachusetts. Two years later he was one of the leaders in a movement to detach the community of Reading from Lynn. That occurred in 1639, and Pearson is regarded as one of the founders of Reading, where he lived the rest of his life. He became a proprietor of the town as early as 1644, was admitted as a freeman May 26, 1647, and held many town offices. He died in Reading April 17, 1679, at the age of 63.

Only with the fifth generation do we find the name changed from Pearson to Persons. Nathan Persons, the son of Nathan Pearson, was born in 1746 and died in 1795. Grace Emily Proctor reports that both Nathans, father and son, served in the Revolutionary War. The elder Nathan was born in 1725 and therefore

---

[29] While we have engaged in substantial genealogical research on the Persons family, our effort has been greatly aided by the work of Grace Emily Proctor. She prepared a complete genealogy on George Ransom Persons that began with the arrival of John Pearson in America in 1637. The material is contained in a leather-bound notebook, beautifully hand-written in ink. George Ransom Persons was a brother of Mildred's father, Joseph Kirk Persons, and virtually all the information in the Proctor book applies also to Mildred's family. The book was owned by George Persons' granddaughter, Mary Clancy, who said she used it as primary evidence to gain entrance into the Daughters of the American Revolution. We visited Miss Clancy in Ishpeming, Michigan, and she mentioned the book. She graciously allowed us to Xerox it.

[30] There is no citation for the clipping containing this information but it is believed to have come from the genealogical columns in the *Boston Transcript*.

[31] Ibid.

would have been at least 51 when he entered military service; the younger Nathan would have been at least 30.

While we know Nathan Pearson was born in Woburn, Massachusetts, we have no data on the birthplaces of his son or grandson. How long they continued to live in the New England area is a question. At some point, however, the grandson (Nathan) moved to upstate New York. His son, Edward Nathan, was born in Henderson, Jefferson County, New York, in 1814.

Edward Nathan Persons

Edward Nathan Persons spent most of his long life on the Great Lakes and its tributary rivers. About his work, Cutter writes: "For fifty years he was a river navigator, and sailed into Chicago when it was a town of but three hundred inhabitants. He witnessed and was an active participant in all the wonderful development of lake craft, from the canoe to the palatial steamer of today."[32] It is apparent that Edward Nathan was present at the creation of the large and complex transportation network of the Great Lakes. Why Cutter identified him as a "river navigator" is unclear. He was a man of the Great Lakes; and other data reveal many years of service as the captain of various vessels. The 1879 Directory of the City of Ogdensburg lists him as a captain.[33]

This seagoing man had two wives. The first, Mary Guile, survived the marriage only by a year, dying in March 1842. They had one child, a boy. After four years as a widower, Edward Nathan wed Mary M. Burditt, whose family was from Vermont. They pledged their vows in Ogdensburg on January 21, 1846. Over a 22-year period, they had five children, the last dying in infancy in 1868. The oldest was George Ransom Persons, who was the target of the genealogical study by Grace Emily Proctor in 1903. Born in 1848, he had moved to Northern Michigan by the time of his marriage in 1885. There he had a substantial career and had success both in business and in civic affairs.

---

[32] William R. Cutter, *Genealogical and Family History of Northern New York*. New York City: Lewis Historical Publishing Co., 1910, 3 vols. Page citation unavailable.
[33] *Mellon's Directory of the City of Ogdensburg, New York, of 1879*. Further publication details not available.

Mildred's Parents: Joseph Kirk Persons and Elizabeth (Bess) James

George's youngest brother was Joseph Kirk Persons, Mildred's father. Ten years younger than his brother, Kirk (as he was typically known) began life in Canton, N.Y., on March 10, 1858. The Ogdensburg city directory for 1879 listed him as a clerk and boarding with his parents.[34] When he was about 22, he followed his brother to Michigan, where he enrolled in the University of Michigan Law School in Ann Arbor. He graduated in 1884, apparently the first in his family to have earned a professional degree.

The family lore is that he met his future wife, Elizabeth (Bess) James, age 21, when she was attending the State Normal School at Ypsilanti, Michigan. (It is now Central Michigan University, and the two institutions are only about 15 miles apart.) Though we do not have data as support, we believe that Bess taught school after graduating from Ypsilanti, which had a two-year curriculum.

The marriage took place in Red Jacket, Michigan, on June 25, 1889. Joseph Hammond James remembers hearing the James family's view that Bess had "made a very good match."[35] Indeed, Kirk had moved from law school to the practice of law in Duluth, Minnesota, which had a prospering economy largely dependent on mining, timber, and shipping. In less than five years he seemed to have established himself professionally.

The James Family and Settlement in Red Jacket

Kirk married into a family of recent migrants who had already achieved considerable affluence. Joseph R., the father, born in Devon, England in 1842, had very likely worked in Devon copper mines before immigrating to Upper Michigan with his wife and infant daughter (Bess) in 1864. (The development of the copper mining industry had begun about 10 years earlier.) He first worked as a machine operator in the copper mines; and it was in Michigan that a son, Joseph Henry James, was born to his wife, Salome Northey (born in 1841 in Launceston, Cornwall, England) in 1868. Salome had two brothers who also migrated to the Upper Peninsula and settled in generally the same area.

---

[34] Ibid.

[35] Joseph Hammond James was born November 23, 1914 and died November 3, 1993. He was a grandson of Joseph R. and Salome James, a son of Joseph Henry James, and a nephew of Bess Persons. Frank[10] talked at length about his memories of the family with Joseph Hammond James on July 4, 1989.

Some time after 1870,[36] the James family moved to Red Jacket, which was a separate government identity at the time but later became a part of Calumet, Michigan. Largely because of money that came from the great Calumet-Hecla mine, Calumet was a special city in Upper Michigan. It was exceedingly prosperous, constructed significant public buildings, and had a thirst for the arts. The opera house there was nationally known. It was a place where ambitious people had considerable opportunity. By the time Bess was in school, Joseph R. and Salome James were operating a successful soda pop bottling plant and were involving themselves in several land transactions.[37] It is possible that Salome brought skills and experiences in the soda pop industry from England because both her brothers prospered in the same business.

The authors have visited Calumet and examined the site where the soda plant stood. The substantial piece of land is now occupied by a fairly large apartment house. Broken glass is still found on the property, according to the current owner. It must have been quite an impressive operation. Mildred, who could not have been more than five, reported that one of the happiest times in her early life was visiting her grandparents. It was a heavenly situation, as she described it, where a young girl could drink all the soda she wanted, then venture into the orchard behind the building, where she could eat cherries to her heart's content. She said her grandfather called the two Persons sisters "my little cherry pickers." Mildred also remembers a very big house, with many large rooms, that was also adjacent to the cherry orchard.

Kirk Sets Up in Duluth, Minnesota and Begins His Family

Like Calumet, the Duluth where Kirk set up his offices was a fast-growing, bustling town in the 1890's. The shipping industry was thriving, the forests were yielding major amounts of timber, and new veins of iron ore were rapidly being discovered. At the beginning of the 20th century, Duluth was very rich. Visit there today (2006), and one cannot help but be impressed by the large number of mansions that grace its hills. Most were built in the 1900-1915 period.

---

[36] The 1870 Census shows the James family at the Copper Falls mine, Keeweenaw county, Michigan. The family members were Joseph R. James, age 27, an engine driver; Salome, a housewife, age 28; Betsy [Bessie], age 7; and Joseph Henry, 2. All but Joseph Henry were identified as English.

[37] Joseph R. James waited 30 years before he announced his intent to become a U.S. citizen on February 2, 1894. He was granted citizenship in 1902. There is no record that Salome ever sought citizenship.

Shortly after their marriage, Kirk and Bess acquired a substantial home north of Duluth's town center, situated on Lake Superior. It was not a mansion but it was a substantial two-story structure that occupied a beautiful site on the water. In 1995 the house still stood and was occupied by a psychologist, practicing locally. The structure did not convey luxury but it seemed a quite proper statement of upward mobility.

There was considerable movement back and forth between Duluth and Calumet. Mildred remembered the enjoyment of taking a ship from Duluth to Calumet. A visit by Bess to see her parents made the social columns of the Calumet newspaper. Two clippings from the *Calumet and Red Jacket News* are illustrative, one appearing just days after the nuptials: "Bessie, the daughter of Mr. Joseph James, formerly of this place but now of Red Jacket on Tuesday last began reading the brochure, 'Is Marriage a Failure?' she having been married on that day."[38] Another clipping a few months later reported: "Mr. Joe James Jr. [sic], who has been visiting St. Paul, Minneapolis, and Duluth, returned on Monday last. He was accompanied by his sister, Mrs. J. K. Persons, who is at present visiting with her parents here."[39]

According to city directories, Kirk occupied offices in the better buildings in Duluth. However, it is far from clear that he devoted his full energies to the practice of law. In 1887-88, for example, he is listed as co-owner of Persons and Loranger, a lumber company.[40] On another occasion he is identified as having his hand in the soda pop business, importing beverages from his in-laws in Calumet. At some point, very likely in the 1890's, he was involved in a paint factory that was enjoying success. The great problem was that his riches went up in smoke. Paint factories in those days were like tinder boxes, exceedingly flammable, and insurance companies would not touch them. One day the factory burned to the ground, and all that was left were

Kirk in his Duluth office with one of his two girls. We think it was Mildred, who idolized him

---

[38] *Calumet and Red Jacket News,* June 28, 1889.
[39] *Calumet and Red Jacket News,* September 20, 1889.
[40] *1887-88 Michigan State Gazeteer and Business Directory,* p. 384.

the ashes. Memories of that sad fire elicited doleful faces many years later in San Diego.

With all this, Kirk seemed still to be making a good living; and he and Bess appeared to move with a large group of ambitious people in Duluth. What they likely had in common was their aspiration for wealth. Mildred recalled, as a little girl, how she and her sister sat at the top of the stairs in their house and ogled the glamorous people who came to their parents' parties. It was different from her grandparents' soda pop factory, but it left an indelible memory. She recalled those times as extremely exciting.

The main game at the time, however, was dealing in mining claims. It was a highly speculative business. Individuals would acquire the mineral rights on a piece of property and hold them in the anticipation that ore would be discovered. If it was, they were rich. If it were not, they held a useless piece of paper. Enough dry holes and the money for such speculation disappeared.

From Bess' reminisces in her old age, essentially all the people in her crowd were lucky. Their claims held ore. As she put it, "They found ore all around our claims." The effect was apparently devastating. In that time and setting, money was everything. If you did not have a lot of it, you really had no identity. You did not count. Even in her old age, Bess was indignant that fortune had not smiled on the Persons family more generously.

The Family Moves and the Adventures Begin

We do not know why Kirk and his family moved from Duluth but there appear to be at least three possible reasons. One was that living with the friends who had become rich was simply intolerable for the Persons as a "keeping up with the Joneses" couple, despite the fact that Kirk continued as a reasonably well compensated lawyer. The second was that Kirk may have succumbed to the mining bug. The mines were beginning to decline in Michigan, and so there may have been a felt need to move elsewhere. Finally, the reality was that Kirk's in-laws, the James, were making the pioneering move to San Diego, California, where they had bought a home in 1905.

The James Family Settles on San Diego, California

What prompted the James move to San Diego can only be conjectured. Joseph R. had a sister who lived for many years in Los Angeles, but we do not know when she arrived there. The shift to San Diego may have been the indirect result of an accident suffered by their son, Joseph Henry. We understand he was involved in a fire where shattered glass had cut his arm from wrist to shoulder.

The injury was severe, and the pain must have been very great. The only relief was morphine, to which Joseph Henry became addicted. In order to cure him, the parents shipped him on a tramp steamer, first to Australia and then to Japan. He was gone for nearly two months, and the time without drugs cured him. It may be that Joseph Henry was the James who discovered San Diego.

The Keeley Cure Disaster

There was one adventure early in the 20th century about which we have little factual knowledge but which we are quite sure occurred. It involved the operation of a Keeley Cure Institute on Park Avenue in New York City. Joseph Hammond James was absolutely certain that the Keeley Cure played an important part in the James family history.[41] For even the not-so-young reader, the Keeley Cure may draw an absolute blank. Today it is difficult to secure any information about it, but for about 30 years, roughly from 1880 to 1910, it was extremely well known and one of the prime means for combating alcoholism. There is a book, published in 1998, that devotes a chapter to Keeley. Entitled "Franchising Addiction Treatment: The Keeley Institutes," it contains the following chapter subheadings: Humble Beginnings of a National Phenomenon; Keeley: On the Causes of Inebriety; The Keeley Patients; The Keeley Staff; The Keeley Treatment; The Mail Order Business; the Keeley Leagues; Reported Treatment Outcomes; Other Gold Cures; Early Controversies and Clinics; Turn of the Century Decline; the Later Keely Years: 1900-1966; the Keeley Legacy.

The home page for Dwight, Illinois, declares it was the place where Dr. Leslie Keeley opened the first Keeley Institute in 1879. It is said to have been the first medical institution to treat alcoholism as a disease. "By the 1890's," it is reported on the Dwight home page, "every state and nearly every country had a Keeley Institute of its own." There is a note at another Internet site from the Palo Alto *Reporter* of Palo Alto, Iowa, that "…Homer Cummins is down to Eagle Grove this week, and the boys and girls say he has gone to take the Keely cure."[42]

Another Internet site reports that

"…addiction treatment programs have been around a lot longer than has generally been recognized. White says the first medically oriented treatment program opened in New York in 1864, and then hundreds of private, for-profit 'Keeley Institutes' sprung up around the country in the 19th century to treat

---

[41] Joseph Hammond James, *op. cit.*
[42] *Palo Alto Reporter*, February 26, 1892

addiction. The Keeley institutes begat the Keeley Leagues, which organized a march on the Pennsylvania capitol to demand treatment in 1894."[43]

The James family appeared to have struck on something that had every prospect of making substantial money. To possess the Keeley franchise on luxurious Park Avenue in New York City certainly seemed to hold great promise. Sadly, though, things were beginning to fall apart by the turn of the century. Perhaps there were too many people trying to make a quick buck. Major skepticism developed about the worth of such treatment programs, and there was a return to thinking of alcoholism as a moral question rather than a medical one.

Thus the family descended on New York City just as things were changing. It is not entirely clear who was involved in the New York city venture. Because of Joseph Hammond James' certainty about his information, it seems likely that this was a James project, involving mother, father, and son Joseph Henry. Frank[10] says he remembers a number of references to the Keeley Cure; and the way members of the family seemed to share the experience made him think everyone was involved. It is a fact, though, that neither Mildred nor her sister Lois ever spoke of being in New York City. One has to conclude that the Persons were not involved.

In any case, the venture was a fiasco. Nothing good was said about the Keeley Cure in the James-Persons household. The infrequent references to it always seemed to generate derision.

The 25th Street House

With the Keeley Cure behind them, the James family moved on to San Diego, where they bought a house at 759-25th street in 1905 and began to invest in real estate. The house was substantial but did not measure up to a number of others in the area, Golden Hill, where development had begun about 1880. It was a beautiful piece of property, with views of open land to the east, bay and ocean to the south, and little slits of water to the west. Just a few blocks to the north was a part of San Diego's massive Balboa Park. With all its attractiveness, Joseph Hammond James reported that his grandfather did not want the house. He desired one closer to the fire station.[44] His desires were met just a few years later when a fire station was constructed two blocks away at 25th street and Broadway.

---

[43] "Join Together", site on the Internet. "Recovery Movement Needs to Keep Distance from Treatment Field," November 16, 2000.
[44] Joseph Hammond James, *op. cit.*

The financing of the 25th street house is interesting. Frank[10] learned about the arrangement in the 1930's in the days of the Great Depression. There was immense fear that the mortgage of $2000 would not be renewed by the people who had held it for many years. The anxiety was understandable because prices had fallen during the Depression so much that the family very likely no longer had any equity. The neighborhood had deteriorated and old houses were a dime a dozen. In a discussion Bess revealed that the house had been purchased in 1905 for $5000; the James family put in $3000 and got a mortgage for $2000 at 6% interest. That mortgage had remained on the house for about 30 years.

Though the 25th street property was purchased in 1905 and there has always been the understanding that the James family moved into the house as soon as construction was completed, ties were not quickly severed in Calumet. From the data we have, it appears that son Joseph Henry stayed in Calumet to operate the bottling business. Joseph Henry James is listed as the manager and operator of Joseph James Bottler from 1902 to 1910. The listings vary slightly, as in these examples: "Joseph H., bottler Joseph James" in 1905 and "Joseph H., manager J. James" in 1902.[45] In the 1909-1910 *Directory* the business was identified as "mineral waters." The family was not listed in the 1911-1912 *Directory.*

Joseph R. James outside the house on 25th street with his great grandchildren, Elizabeth and Frank[10].

The Persons Family in Salt Lake City, Utah

The Persons family maintained their residence in Duluth until about 1907, though they had moved to Salt Lake City, where they stayed about a year. What prompted the move there is not known. About the only thing Frank[10] remembers Bess saying about this part of her life was the degree to which she was

---

[45] We examined *Polk's Calumet Directory*, which was published bi-annually, for the years 1901-1912. We found entries for all the years except 1911-1912. By that time it appeared that the family had completely departed Calumet.

impressed by the buoyancy of the Great Salt Lake. She could not forget how easy it was to float in it. One reason we are fairly certain the family was in Salt Lake comes from the obituary of Kirk's brother, George, who died in 1908. Kirk and his family were said to be in Salt Lake at the time. Also, there is a record that Kirk continued his membership in the Masonic Lodge in Salt Lake. Since the family was both in Salt Lake and in San Diego in 1908, it is probable that they spent part of 1907 in Salt Lake. They talked of being there about a year.

We have no information on Kirk's activities in Salt Lake. There is no evidence he practiced law. It is more probable that his Salt Lake activity involved mining. Indeed, his days of legal practice were over. He was never listed as in the law in San Diego.

Everyone in San Diego

The 1908 San Diego *Directory* places the Persons family in town.[46] Kirk was listed as engaged in mining, and the family residence was at 3758 Fifth Avenue. Their home was in the Hillcrest area and close to Balboa Park, a comfortable, middle-class part of the community. Interestingly, there is no listing for Joseph R. James until 1911, and none at all for Salome. There are many omissions in the *Directory*. Joseph R. James is listed only three times in the eight years between 1908 and 1916; yet we know that he was living on 25th street during that time, except for the year the family was in Ensenada. It seems reasonable to conclude that in 1908 Salome and Joseph R. were residing alone in the big house on 25th street; the Persons were in Hillcrest, and Joseph Henry was still in Calumet. He had divorced his first wife by that time and may have begun a relationship with his second wife, Eva Hammond.

By 1909 Joseph Henry, perhaps with his new wife, was also located in San Diego and living on 25th street. Meanwhile, the Persons had moved and were located a little closer to town, still on Fifth Avenue. Their new address was 2166; and this seemed to be the location of both a mining office and a residence.

In this period Mildred was attending Florence Elementary school, which was located in the Hillcrest area. We have pictures that indicate she was involved in Florence activities and probably enjoying the experience. It happens that she and her son had the same teacher, she at Florence and Frank[10] at Roosevelt Junior High School. The teacher, Leah Colbert, said on more than one occasion, "Frank, you are not nearly as nice a person as your mother." Mildred would have turned

---

[46] *San Diego City-County Directory 1908*. (San Diego: Frye and Smith printers, 1908)

14 in November 1909; and, because of the time in Salt Lake, she may have lost some academic standing. In the Florence school pictures, though, she looks about the same age as her fellow students.

Silver Mining in Ensenada, Mexico

As she finished at Florence, Mildred and her sister were destined to enter on a very unhappy time. Their father decided that the whole family should explore for silver in Ensenada, Mexico.

This Mexican town, then no more than a small village on the Pacific Ocean, is about 85 miles south of San Diego. In those days there were no good roads; it was necessary to travel by sea.

These ladies are not happy campers at Ensenada, Mexico. From left Lois, Salome, Mildred, and a Mrs. Todd.

This was a major undertaking and we think it took place primarily in 1910. That was a year when there were no family listings in the *San Diego Directory*.

The venture involved a number of people and lasted about a year. Not only were the four Persons involved but also Joseph R. and Salome James. Joseph Henry James may have been present because his son, Joseph Hammond, reported that he spent time in Mexico and developed a reasonable facility with the language. At one time there were voluminous records and pictures, all stored in the basement of the 25th street house. They were lost. All we have left are four pictures of Ensenada life.

This was not the Ritz. One gets the impression, though, that the project involved major capital investment. One picture shows lumber being hauled to a shaft entrance. It is hard to believe that the undertaking did not include a considerable amount of Persons money. Another picture shows the tents in which they lived; and another portrays four disconsolate Persons-James women.

For the two girls (Mildred would have been 15 and Lois 19), the stay in Ensenada was a disaster. They both described it as the worst year of their lives. Beyond all the hardships and inconveniences, it meant a year away from school. And, of course, there was no social scene. Lois withdrew from high school in January 1909 and never went back. She was 18 at the time, and it may be she left school quite separately from the Ensenada venture. In Mildred's case, it was a serious interruption in her schooling and may have been compounded by lost time in Salt Lake. In any case, the records show that she entered San Diego High School in January 1912 with advanced standing as a 9th grader. Curiously, she was shown as having completed the first 9th grade semester at "Normal School." We have no idea what that institution was. When she entered San Diego High, she had just passed her 16th birthday, certainly old for a 9th grader. The school, incidentally, showed her born in 1896, rather than 1895, an error she might have made purposely because she was old for her grade. Mildred quit San Diego high on January 31, 1914, after her 18th birthday. She always said she left at the end of the 10th grade, but these records show she completed the first semester of the 11th.

The Ensenada Fiasco and Its Consequences

It is probable that the damage done to Mildred's education was the lesser of the problems the Persons faced on returning to San Diego. The search for silver in Ensenada failed completely, and it was regarded as another financial debacle, similar to the Keeley Cure. That the Ensenada trip left the Persons family in severe financial straits is suggested by the fact that they moved into their in-laws' house on 25th street when they returned, as did Joseph Henry James. Everyone was now under the same roof, and it is assumed that Salome and Joseph R. were in control. It is somewhat revealing that the two parents had the best room in the house, a front one with large windows, and Kirk and Bess had a smaller, much less impressive room in the rear of the house. Joseph R. retained his room as long as he lived; and Bess stayed in hers for the rest of her life.

The increased reliance on the James assets could have permanently diminished Kirk's role and status in the family. Eva Hammond James, who lived for a number of years with her husband in the 25th street house, commented to her son, Joseph Hammond, that Salome was the "brains of the family." She said that Salome "...invested in the only thing she knew, property"[47] Our research on earlier property transactions in Calumet seemed to support Eva's observation. We found that the James family was fairly heavily involved in real estate; and the signatory in the transactions was typically Salome.[48]

---

[47] Joseph Hammond James, *op. cit.*
[48] We have the records of these Calumet transactions but do not consider them of sufficient importance to include them here.

Salome Dies and the Family Power Structure Changes

The death of Salome on June 8, 1912, was undoubtedly a major blow. A short newspaper obituary contained few details and said nothing about the cause of her death.[49] She had a heart condition and a liver problem.

Salome's passing probably did not create legal problems. She was a spouse, and Joseph R. now was in sole possession of James family assets. If, as appears to be the case, Salome handled the financial affairs, there was the question who would take over. Joseph R. did not seem to be a financial person. When Frank[10] came on the scene as a small child a little more than a decade later, he remembers his great grandfather fondly but not as a powerful figure in the family. He cannot recall a time in the following seven years when Joseph R. was involved in a discussion about money.[50] The successor was Bess. There can be little doubt that she was in charge of the finances of the family from 1912 to her death in 1943. While Joseph R. was regarded as someone whose care was highly important, beyond that he was a presence and not a participant in significant family matters.

Bess did have a brother, of course, and that suggested an issue of inheritance would subsequently develop. That question was resolved, however, by the early death of Joseph Henry James on June 1, 1930 at the age of 61. Joseph R. outlived his son by two years, passing away at the age of 89 on February 10, 1932. At that time Frank[10] cannot remember anything being said about passing some of the property to Eva and her son. Bess was in complete charge of the assets, which may well have been put in her name, and things continued as they had for the past 20 years.

It is unclear how Kirk was faring economically in this period. The 1911 San Diego *Directory* lists Bess as living on 25th street, but there is no mention of Kirk, either in terms of residence or business. He does appear in the 1912 *Directory* as a partner in the real estate firm of Krider and Persons, at 1126-6th Avenue, fairly close to the downtown area. There is no further mention of an involvement in mining.

---

[49] *San Diego Union,* June 9, 1912, p. 15. It stated, "In this city, June 8, 1912, Salome James, wife of Joseph James and mother of Joseph H. James and Mrs. J.K. Persons of San Diego, a native of England, aged 71 years, 3 mos. and 29 days. Announcement of funeral services will be made later by Johnson, Connelle, and Saum."

[50] It should not be assumed that Joseph R. was without an interest in money. He liked the things it bought. Joseph Hammond James remembers being told that his grandfather always had his shirts hand-made in Chicago. The manufacturer once wrote Joseph R. saying that he was its oldest customer. Suits were also tailored. And, when travel by train was involved, he and Salome carried a personal tea set with them. It is reported that they always drank Oolong tea.

Joseph Henry James also appears in the 1912 *Directory*. He was in the cigar business at 1332 F street, about 12 blocks west of the 25th street house, where he resided. The F street address was not a retail area and it is likely he had a warehouse operation there. His son, Joseph Hammond, reported that his father ran a chain of cigar stores. It was also said in the family that Joseph Henry and Kirk ran a tobacco and periodicals counter in one of the larger office buildings in town, at 5th and E streets. However, the various *Directories* do not list this as an activity of either man. What occurred in the following year is not known. We could not find a 1913 *Directory*.

Ocean Beach Property

Before she died, we believe Salome had begun investing in Ocean Beach, a San Diego suburb on the ocean. In the first two decades of the 20th century, Ocean Beach was the getaway for San Diegans. It prospered. The area was north of Point Loma, the huge and rocky promotory that rose up from the sea and created the San Diego Harbor. From the sands of Ocean Beach, one could walk a short distance south and be among the rocks and crashing waters of Point Loma, in an area called Sunset Cliffs. It was quite a wonderful spot. What helped Ocean Beach to achieve its ascendancy was the time and difficulty getting to other beach areas.

The easiest to reach would have been Mission Beach, a narrow spit of land that extended south from the mainland and formed the western rampart for a large body of water originally called False Bay and then Mission Bay. The original name came because explorers thought at first it was the real San Diego Bay. While it was large, it was shallow—wonderful for recreation but not for shipping. The bay's expanse was so great that it was a long trip just to encircle it and approach Mission Beach from the north. The problem was that a narrow cut existed between Ocean Beach and Mission Beach through which tides moved ceaselessly from ocean to bay and back again Thus, except with a boat, Mission Beach was not easily accessible.

Not surprisingly, it was on the south side (the Ocean Beach side closest to San Diego) that an amusement park, Wonderland, was built and prospered for many years. Ocean Beach also boasted a large dance hall and a large but unpretentious salt water swimming pool, the Crystal Plunge.

Before she died, Salome had purchased three pieces of property, two of them adjoining business lots on Newport Avenue just a few doors east of the dance hall, which was on the beach. Later, one of these lots housed a small store and the other a fairly large building. The other acquisition was a residential property about four blocks from Newport Avenue and about a block from the ocean. When Frank[10] knew the house in the mid-1920's, it was reasonably old, probably built in the early part of the century. It was an attractive redwood home of about 1000 square feet, with its biggest attraction the porch that spanned the entire front. The planter boxes on the solid railing were particularly appealing. There was no front yard; the house abutted the sidewalk on Abbott street. It was definitely beach property.

Frank[10] remembers a few occasions when the family spent time at Ocean Beach. These excursions were much too few, probably because none of the older people seemed to have an interest in the beach. The house was usually rented and was sold in the 1930's.

The 1914 *Directory* revealed that both Kirk and Joseph Henry had made Ocean Beach their base of operations. Kirk had opened a real estate office on Newport Avenue, very likely in the small store the family owned. Joseph Henry had embarked on a more major undertaking. He and his wife Eva were operating a movie house, the Ocean Theater, in the large building the James family owned. Where Kirk commuted to Ocean Beach from 25th street, Joseph and Eva moved there. It appears that the real estate business in Ocean Beach was not particularly successful. The 1915 *Directory* lists no business identification; and in 1916 Kirk is identified as a clerk. In 1917 the identification was once again with mining. Later, Frank[10] did ask what his grandfather did during the war and was told that Kirk was a "night watchman."

Meanwhile, the Ocean Theater, from all accounts, seems to have done well. Joseph and Eva are listed as operating there through 1919, though they moved back to the 25th street house in 1916. This fairly primitive silent film house, though, had a short life. By 1920 it was clear the movies were here to stay, and there was money to made in operating a theater. Investors constructed the far more elaborate Strand Theater a block further east on Newport Avenue, and that spelled the end of the Ocean Theater.

The Decline of Ocean Beach

Ocean Beach, too, lost its special attraction shortly after World War I. A bridge was constructed across the cut that separated Ocean and Mission Beach. The Mission Beach peninsula was now easily accessible and had miles of waterfront frontage, both on the ocean and on the bay. Its attractions were many, and all the facilities of a major resort community were erected, dwarfing Ocean Beach. Wonderland was soon razed, and the dance hall in Ocean Beach stood vacant for many years before a final demolition. The Crystal Plunge remained for a time but it could not compete with the larger, beautifully tiled salt water plunge in Mission Beach. Ocean Beach's place in the sun had ended and so the James properties plummeted in value.

Big Changes in Mildred's Life: Becoming an RN and Marriage

As Kirk was setting up his real estate office and "Uncle Joe" was running two-reel films in the Ocean theater, Mildred was departing on her own great adventure. When she quit San Diego high school in January 1914, she began nurse's training at San Diego's Agnew hospital. She had just turned 18.

In Training at Agnew Hospital

While there appears to be little information on the Agnew and its history, we are fortunate in having Mildred's photograph album, which contains pictures of many of the nurses in training and also provides some sense of the structure. It was the first hospital training school for nurses in San Diego, established in 1900. [51] Its first graduating class numbered five; the class of 1909 had 19; and the last, in 1919, totaled 18. From the pictures, it appeared that Mildred's class, which would have graduated in 1917, was about the same size.

Fosbinder quotes an alumna of Agnew that the training was "strict," and that it involved "three long, hard years." She reported that women "....swelled with pride when any doctor said, 'I can tell you are an Agnew girl.'"[52] Reunions were held by graduates for many years, with a dominant theme their real enjoyment of their hard work together. Fosbinder emphasizes that the nurse trainees had to labor very long hours, took on the most menial tasks, and got little recognition for their efforts. Trainees received $25 per week to work 20 hour shifts. But Mildred's pictures reveal that the women did get time off, at least enough to have some fun moments in the hospital.

Mildred sits on the Agnew Hospital roof. In the background can be seen houses in the area.

---

[51] Donna Fosbinder, "Hospital Based Nursing Schools in San Diego, 1900-1970," *The Journal of San Diego History*, 5:110,113 (Spring, 1989). This essay may be the only resource on the history of the Agnew.
[52] Ibid.

Clearly, marriage and men were very much on the minds of these attractive young women. Mildred's best friend, Beth Jones, is labeled "the vamp" in her photograph album. Mildred identifies herself as the "old maid," and there is another picture of six nurses, called the "old maids' tatting society." Another girl is identified as the "modest violet." Mildred gave her son numerous accounts of escapades in the hospital days, virtually all of them unfortunately forgotten. One does remain, however. It involved a young woman with very large breasts, seemingly out of style in the emerging flapper period. There was consensus among the trainees that the breasts should be taped down for an impending date. They were taped, and the young lady went off with her young man. She was soon back, however, and was in agony. The tape had to come off. Then another problem ensued. The tape was tightly stuck to the skin. It was a long time before that girl got comfortable again.

The service station Kirk operated for about six years, from 1919 to 1925, was in the heart of the Hillcrest business district. See footnote 53.

Agnew was about 120 miles from Hollywood, which was then becoming the film capital of the nation. Agnew was just far enough way to escape prying eyes and offered a refuge for the wild bunch engaged in making movies. Two of the famous figures to spend time at Agnew were Charlie Chaplin and Fatty Arbuckle. They both suffered from venereal disease, and Mildred had nothing good to say about either of them. They clearly violated her moral code.

The Agnew hospital, which was located on Fifth Avenue just north of town, closed in 1919 when it was sold and converted to an apartment house. Frank[10] remembers the building as very large, a brick mass, that was probably better suited as a hospital than an apartment house. It was razed after World War II.

Mildred Named Head of the Infirmary at Hercules Potash Plant;
Romance with Clarence[9] MacKinlay Begins

Not long after the receipt of her certification as a Registered Nurse, Mildred became head of the infirmary at the Hercules Potash Plant, where she encountered Clarence[9] and fell in love with him. It is clearly evident from the photographs in our collection that they liked each other and enjoyed being together. While Mildred is often caught laughing in her Agnew photos, Clarence[9] seldom cracks a smile in his earlier photos. In their pictures of each other during the courting period, happiness radiates on both faces. There was clearly something going on.

While the factor of physical attraction cannot be discounted, it is possible that they sensed a different kind of world together. The record indicates that both were outgoing, gregarious, and social. They did not enjoy confinement, either because of social taboos or family isolation. In previous chapters we have described Clarence[9]'s family experience as one of great love but within an environment of extreme restrictions on individual behavior. He chose to handle that problem by leaving home at age 17 and never really going back.

Mildred's situation was somewhat different but nevertheless confining. While she experienced great love, family life had become increasingly insular. The situation in San Diego was far different from that she had seen as a small child in Duluth. In San Diego there were no family friends, no social occasions with others, and a low level of trust of outside people. The family was everything. This was a style dictated by Bess because Mildred characterized Kirk as always outgoing and engaging. His social inclinations, however, had to be satisfied outside the home.[53] Bess had many strong prejudices toward Catholics, Mexicans, Italians, garlic, and shellfish. For a woman who was wonderful in many ways, she was a real bigot.

Very likely Mildred felt herself living in a family filled with a love but restricted to those few who were inside.[54] Undoubtedly, the move to Agnew was an eye-opener. Her pictures reveal a penchant for social interaction and an affection for all those non-family people who were part of a much larger and more vibrant group.

---

[53] About the time Mildred and Clarence[9] were involved with each other, Kirk was embarking on a new enterprise. In the 1919 city *Directory* he is listed as having a gasoline/auto accessories business in the Hillcrest area of San Diego. It was an early gasoline station, which he operated successfully for the next six years. By 1925 the property, which was at the center of the Hillcrest business district, had simply become too valuable for this kind of use. The owners refused to renew Kirk's land lease. He was out of business. In those times in 1924-25, Frank[10] remembers visiting his grandfather at the station and finding it an extremely hospitable place. Kirk clearly had lots of friends and enjoyed the activity immensely.

[54] Writing about Persons family dynamics is complicated and contradictory. While he recognized her prejudices, Frank[10] found Bess open, easy to deal with, and lots of fun. When he was in college he felt free to have friends stay with him. He had a few parties at 25th street, and there was no one more supportive and helpful than Bess.

It is possible that Clarence[9] and Mildred were enthused about creating a new family that would be far different in orientation, style, and outlook from their previous experiences. Undoubtedly they saw love as the core ingredient in family life. They had both grown up with plenty of that.

Brief Time in Wilmington, Delaware

Mildred always spoke fondly of the time in Wilmington, Delaware, with Clarence[9], but there was nothing she reported that remains in the memory of son Frank[10]. The time there was relatively short. As was stated earlier, Clarence[9] may have been on duty at his new assignment in Brunswick, Georgia, as early as February, 1920.

Clarence[9] with "Sonny" in Brunswick in 1922.

And Then the Move to Brunswick, Georgia

Undoubtedly, the most significant event in Brunswick was the birth of their child, Frank[10] Persons Sherwood, which occurred on October 11, 1920. He was to have been the first of five children, as Mildred commented numerous times. There were several pictures of mother and father doting on "Sonny."

Clarence[9] and Mildred apparently settled easily and enjoyably into Brunswick life. In 2006 the Hercules plant was still a dominant element in the cityscape, and the surrounding area had become an increasingly important tourist attraction. Jekyll Island, which could reached only by boat in the 1920's and was a special preserve of the very, very wealthy, now is accessible by causeway from the mainland. Now, there are many hotels to which visitors can repair and enjoy the scenic waters of the Atlantic. Also just a short drive from Brunswick is St. Simon's Island, where history and urban development link. The Cloisters, one of the great hotels in the world, is located there.

The city of Brunswick, on the other hand, has seen better days. The area in which Clarence[9] and Mildred lived lies south of the downtown and is now referred to as "old Brunswick." The area is being rediscovered because it does have an inherent charm. It was laid out along the lines of Savannah, Georgia. Instead of the usual grid pattern of streets, a series of small squares intersect the road system, providing scenic interest and pocket parks. Many of the large old homes are being restored to some of their former elegance.

While they lived among the well-to-do, the Sherwoods had a much more modest home on one of the side streets, at 918 Egmont. It was a two-story wood house, fairly generous in its proportions, but it did not rival the grand homes around it.

Aside from their preoccupation with their son, the Sherwoods led a life markedly different from those of either of their parents. Mildred described many times the pleasures of their social life in Brunswick. Two obituaries in the Brunswick newspaper show how open and joyful their lives were. One states, "Mr. and Mrs. Sherwood soon took a prominent place in Brunswick's social circles. He was a genial, affable young man who made friends with all with whom he was thrown in contact."[55] The second article, which reported the departure of the body for New York, said this: "No young man ever came to Brunswick who so rapidly won a place in the esteem and affection of his fellows as did Mr. Sherwood. Of a genial, happy disposition, he scattered sunshine wherever he was, and his genial companionship was much sought after. He loved his friends, he idolized his wife and baby. His death comes as a staggering blow..."[56]

Mildred did make one trip to California, in 1922. The purpose was to show her folks their new grandson. Pictures taken during that trip show a happy Mildred and her son cavorting at the beach at Del Mar with her sister and her niece.

The Death of Clarence[9]

It was not long after Mildred's return that Clarence[9] fell ill. It was reported that the illness hit him quite suddenly, and he was dead within four months. There was consensus in the family that Clarence[9] suffered from pancreatic cancer, from which his brother Rosevelt had died four years earlier. However, the death certificate declared the cause as stomach cancer. Mildred never quite accepted these diagnoses and insisted that he could have inadvertently poisoned himself. Litmus paper had not been discovered by chemists in 1923; and the way many

---

[55] This report is obviously from the local Brunswick newspaper, whose name we do not have. It is fairly clear, however, that the date of the report is March 6, 1923, the day after the death of Clarence[9].

[56] This quotation comes from the same newspaper and likely appeared a couple of days later.

substances were identified was by taste. Mildred felt he may have had the bad luck of ingesting something that was poisonous.

Throughout the profoundly painful months of sickness, Clarence[9] was nursed by Mildred. For much of that time he was at home but was finally transferred to the hospital. [We have a problem here because the newspaper declares he went to the hospital on Saturday, March 24, whereas he died on March 5.][57] The experience was excessively traumatic for Mildred. She declared that she could never again be a nurse—and she was not.

Frank[8] and Catherine Anne Sherwood came from Albany to be with Clarence[9] a few days before his death. Also, Lois Carter was present to give support to Mildred. A "short service" was held at the house on Egmont street, preparatory to the shipment of the casket to Albany, New York. The newspaper reports that the casket was borne from the funeral car to the train by eight close friends, and there was "…a wealth of exquisite floral offerings, tokens of the love and esteem in which Clarence McKinley Sherwood was held in the hearts of hundreds of friends, who are sorely grieved over his untimely death."[58]

Clarence[9] was buried at the cemetery in Fort Plain, New York, a town from which Frank[8] had retired as the Methodist minister 10 years earlier. It was the resting place for his brother Rosevelt and would be for his mother and father.

Family Finances

As was reported in an earlier chapter, Clarence[9] kept meticulous financial records. From this journal it is apparent that his marriage in December 1918 created an incentive to develop an estate for his wife and future family. He had, however, begun saving before that. By the end of 1918 and roughly at the time of his marriage, he owned $3850 in Liberty Bonds and a new $1250 automobile. It is probable that at least some of the bonds were cashed, in order to buy a house in Brunswick. We do not have records showing ownership of the Egmont residence, but Mildred gave Frank[10] the impression it was an unmortgaged possession. Other money went to the building of a stock and bond portfolio. That started in 1919 with the purchase of three shares of San Diego Gas and Electric Co. at a total cost of $304.

---

[57] Clarence[9] died on Monday, March 5, 1923. The newspaper was right in stating that March 24 was Saturday.
[58] Second obituary in Brunswick newspaper, probably published about March 8, 1923.

Three other stock purchases were made on February 1, 1920, which was about the time Clarence[9] must have arrived in Brunswick: one preferred share of U.S. Rubber, for $115.50; one preferred share of the Santa Fe railroad, $79.12; and four preferred shares of General Motors, $325.50. All told, the investment in these equities was about $825. He also bought a Baltimore and Ohio Railroad bond for $315.31, which he sold in September 1920 for a $30 profit. A Great Northern Railway bond was purchased, perhaps in 1922, for $510.23.

His largest investment, however, was in Hercules Powder, which had an installment stock purchase plan for its employees. He seems to have paid fully for 24 shares, from 1920 to 1922. Interestingly, the cost of the stock varied between $107 per share (for the first 4 shares) to $90 for the last five shares, which suggests the market was not going in the right way. As carefully as can be calculated, the total value of his Hercules stock was about $2000.

It appears that the size of his estate, not including the equity in the house and in any insurance policies, was a little less than $3500. Mildred sold these equities shortly after his death, probably leaving her with about $10,000 from all sources. It is a tribute to Clarence[9.] that he had done so well in building an estate in such a short time, but it certainly was not enough to leave his widow financially comfortable. Even if the money were exceptionally well invested, the income from it would not pay living expenses. Mildred had to go to work.

Back to San Diego

After a short stay in Albany with her grieving in-laws, Mildred headed back to California to try to put together a very broken life. To move ahead in the story, it must be said that she never really succeeded. She had little interest in other men and did not come close to marrying again. Mildred was never able to find an economic place for herself in a world dominated by men and where she was emotionally unable to return to the professional activity for which she had been trained. With all these disappointments, the wonder is that Mildred kept her good spirits and optimism, and she certainly did not insist that her son share in the sadness she most certainly felt.

The situation in San Diego, to which she returned in 1923, had changed.[59] There were now only three people living on 25th street, Bess and Kirk Persons

---

[59] The arrival at the 25th street house on a bright, sunny day constitutes Frank[10]'s first memory. He remembers it as joyous. Mildred was glad to be home, and her parents and sister were delighted to see her.

and Joseph R. James. Joseph Henry James, wife Eva, and young son Joseph Hammond had left San Diego and were living in Camarillo, California, a small community north of Los Angeles.[60] Her sister Lois had married Ross S. Carter, a physician, long before World War I and had a daughter born in 1915. They lived in a small home in the eastern part of San Diego.

On Their Own About Two Years

One thing was clear. Mildred did not want to live with her parents. She was nearly 28, had been the mistress of her own home, and had enjoyed a life vastly different from that in the house controlled by her mother.

The real question was how she would support herself away from her parents. To begin the process of establishing her independence, she bought two pieces of property in the same Golden Hill area where her parents lived. One was a reasonably modern duplex at 26th and A streets. Her plan was that she and Frank[10] would live on one side, with the other rented. The plan was followed, and mother and son lived in the duplex for two years, from which site he entered Brooklyn elementary school and completed kindergarten and the first grade.

Mildred bought another single family house, about a block and a half west of the duplex, for purely rental purposes. It was an older structure, not in terribly good shape. While it sat on a nice lot, there was little landscaping. It looked neglected. Today, we would say this was a "fixer upper." It was not in the Persons-James culture, however, for the men to perform as handymen. Nobody was about to undertake manual labor, and so the house was rented at a rate that reflected its condition.

But this was not the worst part of things. The conditions of purchase were the real problem. While we do not have information on the duplex, Mildred did write in Clarence[9]'s journal that she had purchased the rental house for $3500, putting down $1700 and assuming a mortgage at 7% for $1800. So far so bad. The kicker was that the mortgage was due in six months. There is every likeli-

---

[60] We do not know the circumstances surrounding the departure. Frank[10] was told on more than one occasion that Bess did not like Eva. But it may also have been that there was an attractive opportunity in Camarillo. There Joseph Henry and Eva ran a large soda fountain and short order cafe that catered to passengers on the Pickwick stages, the largest bus company in California at the time. Frank[10] remembers the fountain as very large and nicely tiled. It seemed to be a prosperous business; but it was not clear who owned it. The James family lived in a small house behind the store.

hood that the same kind of purchase arrangement was made on the duplex, which probably cost $5500-6000. She had used half her assets to buy the two properties and still owed $5000, due almost immediately. Such financing seems incredible today, where essentially all mortgages are amortized over 30 years. If such financing had been available in those days, Mildred would likely have owned that real estate throughout much of her life.

In the mid-1920s, however, the handwriting was on the wall. There was no way she could maintain the houses over any real time span. The properties were lost to the bankers by the end of 1926. She had no alternative but to move back in with her parents. Frank[10] remembers a rude awakening at that time. He was in a store with Mildred and making his usual demand that she buy something for him. There was great sadness on her face as she said, "Frank, I can't buy anything for you. I have only $7 in the bank." Frank[10] has never forgotten that moment. Even at his early age, he found her statement chilling, and he could see how difficult it was for her to deal with this reality

Deaths in the Family

Kirk was First

The year 1926 brought tragedy to 25th street. Kirk, always the picture of health, suffered a massive stroke. It left an entire side of his body paralyzed, made speech very difficult, and affected his mind. He was a shell of what he had been. To a young Frank[10] there was no sadder sight than to see his grandfather drag himself along the sidewalk in front of the house. Kirk survived in this deteriorated state for about two years, dying on May 4, 1928. He had just passed his 70th birthday.

And It Required Bess to Learn to Drive at Age 60

Kirk's stroke created a major transportation problem in the family. Although two streetcar lines were available within two blocks, the auto had become the way of getting around town. Life depended on the ability to visit the public library at 8th and E streets at least twice a week; to access the major, open air markets on 12th street, about a mile away, even oftener; and to visit the harbor for fish at least once a week. With Kirk unable to drive, there were only Bess, Joseph R., (then 83), and Mildred, who had to work. Lois, who lived in the eastern part of town, did not drive.

In her typical fashion, Bess decided there was nothing but to learn to drive. She was 60. The car she learned to handle, and for which she received a license,

Kirk in the 1920's

was one you cannot find today. It was a Model T Ford, the one which Henry Ford had pioneered and on which he made his first millions. Nearly all cars at the time had a clutch, which required synchronization between clutching and shifting. Bess had doubts about her skills in handling such a clutch. There were, of course, no vehicles with automatic transmissions. Thus she settled on the Model T, which had two instead of three gears. It was controlled by three foot pedals: a brake, which you pushed in to stop the car; a clutch, which you pressed in fully to move the car forward in its lower gear and let out to ascend to the high gear; and a smaller pedal between the other two which you pressed to put the car in reverse. Acceleration was handled by a lever on the steering column. Bess became a master of her Model T and drove it for more than 15 years, into her middle 70s.

Joseph Henry James Was the Second to Go

As has been previously reported, Joseph Henry James, Bess' brother, died in 1930. A year or so after his death, Joseph Hammond James enlisted in the U.S. Navy, was a participant in World War II, and retired in about 1960. In 1939, he married his second cousin, Lois Elizabeth Carter, the daughter of Ross and Lois Carter, and Bess' granddaughter. They had three children and were together for about 20 years until Lois Elizabeth died April 7, 1959.

His Father Followed Him Two Years Later

Joseph R. James suffered a fate very similar to that of his son-in-law, Kirk. He also had a massive stroke that paralyzed half his body, and he similarly lingered with his disability for two years. He died February 10, 1932.

After his death, the residents of the 25th street house were Bess, Mildred, and Frank[10]. By this time economic conditions were really harsh. The stock market crash had occurred in 1929, and things had gone down ever since. The vote for Franklin Roosevelt and against Herbert Hoover in 1932 largely turned on what happened in the economy. It was after FDR had taken office in March 1933 that the bank holiday was declared. That was an eery time. To walk around town and see shuttered banks, most of them in grand buildings with marble everywhere, certainly did nothing to inspire confidence in the future.

Largely because of the economy, Lois and her family moved to 25th street in later 1932. They had been living in a nice, fairly upscale home north and a little east of town. Her husband, Ross Carter, was suffering from the economic disaster that gripped the nation. Though a well-known physician who had practiced about 20 years and was exceedingly well credentialed with a degree from the Johns Hopkins Medical School, he was finding it very difficult to make a living. Patients were simply not coming to him. Of those who did, he reported that he realized cash from only about half his fee billings. As he described it, one third of the patients simply did not pay, a third did, and the final third paid only through bill collectors, who pocketed half the amount due.

Plenty of space existed at 25th street, and renting their house helped the Carters make ends meet. While there would be no rent at 25th street, a significant contribution to the food bills was made by the Carters. In those days these arrangements made a lot of economic sense. Nobody thought much about their own space.

There was another reason for the move. It will be recalled that, after moving to San Diego in 1908, the family appeared to close itself off to outsiders. Lois had only two close friends, her mother and her sister. Her daughter, Lois Elizabeth (always known as Pose in the family) was a senior in high school, striking out on her own, and without the best of relations with her parents. She continued to live at 25th street, however, until she married her second cousin, Joseph Hammond James, in 1939. For Lois the move to 25th street meant a close, day-long association with Bess and frequent contact with sister Mildred. While her husband and daughter were important to her, it is striking that this warm and friendly person was heavily dependent on her mother and sister for her social interaction.

Bess, the Matriarch, Dies in 1943

The close association between mother and daughters continued for the next 11 years until Bess' death on June 1, 1943. She had a massive heart attack and essentially dropped dead. Bess' death was a tremendous blow to both sisters, but most particularly to Lois. Not only had she lost a dear companion but she grieved that she had been insensitive to her mother's worsening health. Over the years she and Bess had developed a give and take relationship that was perhaps more characteristic of sisters than of a mother and daughter. Lois felt she had not given her aging, ailing mother the nurturing that Bess deserved and would have received had her precarious health been known. With a doctor in the house, the question might be asked why there was no such warning. Lois' husband, Ross, said he saw the telltale signs but there was no medical answer to the problem. A serious heart condition was considered absolutely fatal in those days. He chose not to say anything, particularly to his wife, because he thought everyone would be better off treating Bess as a fully functioning individual, rather than as an invalid.

Frank[10] was in Washington, D.C. at the time and made an effort to get home for the funeral. But it was wartime. A civilian had no standing. Needless to say, he did not make it.

The Great Influence of Both Mother and Grandmother on Frank[10]

Bess lives sharply today in Frank[10]'s memory. She was not only a wonderful grandmother but a good, frequently playful, friend. And she was always a supporter. Where she tended to tell her daughters what she thought they should do, she was much more inclined to let Frank[10] figure things out for himself, and then announce she was in his corner.

Vignettes about Bess and Her Specialness

She, of course, played a big part in raising her grandson. Her more detached wisdom was a significant counterpart to Mildred's emotional, heavily involved feelings for her son. Once, when Frank[10] was about eight, he had a major quarrel with his mother and announced that he was leaving home. Mildred was in tears, whereas Bess offered her support to him. "If you insist on going," she counseled, "you should take some lunch with you." He appreciatively agreed, the food was placed in a container, and Grandma helped Frank[10] strap it to the carrier on his bicycle, as a melancholy Mildred stood by. Frank[10] rolled his bike out to 25th street and took off to

Bess in old age

the north, toward the firehouse. "Now, I want you to come up to my room," Bess said to Mildred. From her window in the back of the house, the two could watch a young boy turn right at the firehouse, ride east on Broadway for a very long block, then turn right on 26th street and travel four blocks to Market street, where he again turned right. He was coming home. He could be seen riding along Market and headed for 25th street. There he was lost from sight, but it was clear he would show up at the house in a few minutes. Bess and Mildred were there to welcome him home. Nothing more was said. Much, much later Bess explained to Frank[10] exactly how his journey had been tracked.

When Frank[10] had his 16th birthday, Bess spent rather lavishly on him. She bought him a silk dressing gown that he coveted because that is what leading men in the movies often wore. It is a piece of apparel he still has, 69 years later. Bess also paid for a night on the town. For the first time she, Mildred and Frank[10] went to the Café of the World, a popular restaurant in Balboa Park, the entertainment center of the California Pacific International Exposition, a major fair then completing its second and last year. The evening went beautifully. It was a lot of fun and was highlighted by a floor show, the featured attraction being a fan dancer, at the time required in any club that even pretended to have a floor show. At the end of her act, after many suggestive moves, the dancer flung her fans into the air, at which time Bess exclaimed, "My God, she's got no clothes on!" The dancer did, of course, but with the lighting and distance, there was certainly the impression that we were observing a nude woman. After recovering from her surprise, Bess went on enjoying herself. She did not condone nudity but she was not going to let it interfere with a thoroughly pleasant evening with her daughter and grandson.

The dressing gown was not the only evidence of her generosity. At another point early in his life, Bess bought Frank[10] an Elgin watch in a white gold case, then second only to Hamilton as the desired American watch. Even Mildred thought the purchase was unwise. She felt her son was too young to take proper care of such an expensive item. Frank[10], of course, had a different take. The present was further evidence of his grandmother's confidence in him. She was again right. He wore that watch through college and lost it when he was in the Army.

In a cabinet full of beautiful cut glass that had been assembled by the family over a period of 60 or more years, there was a very large punch bowl. It truly dominated the collection; and, over the years, Frank[10] developed a tremendous attachment to it. While all her property was divided equally between her two daughters, Bess specified that the punch bowl was to go to Frank[10]. In 2006 it still sits in the center of the Sherwood china cabinet.

There was one intimate moment when Bess revealed herself to Frank[10] in a way she may not have to anyone else. The discussion topic itself was quite unexciting. She had suggested, somewhat wistfully, that perhaps the two of them could go into the service station business together. The idea was on its face ridiculous. The grandmother was close to 75 and the boy was about 18. Then she said, "If I had it do over again, I would never get married." Frank[10] did not take the comment to mean that she was rejecting her family. Rather, it was a wish that she could have done something more challenging and more rewarding with her life. Today, there is no doubt that she would have been a top flight business woman, and she probably would have been able to balance family and career. One wonders how many "Besses" have been frustrated because of the chauvinistic world in which they lived.

With Bess' death the Persons family was a thing of the past. From the perspective of Frank[10], of course, Mildred will always be a central figure. It has seemed useful to write enough about the Persons family to convey a sense of the environment in which the lone member of the tenth generation of Sherwoods developed and matured. Mildred introduced a new set of genes into the Sherwood family tree. But this is a book about the Sherwood line; the story of the Persons and James families deserves extensive treatment elsewhere.

Mildred: the Central Figure in Frank's Early Life

The story of Mildred's widowhood and later experience reflect the vicissitudes of a life profoundly affected by the loss of a loved one and is contained in Appendix One.

It would be remiss, however, not to indicate here a sense of the profound relationship between Frank[10] and his mother.

In many ways the long distance communication with his mother during Frank[10]'s Army service in 1943-46 showed the depth of the tie between mother and son. Mindful of Civil War letters, Frank[10] asked Mildred to keep all the correspondence he sent her. She faithfully retained all of them, and they now constitute a 400-page volume, which reposes in several libraries.[61] What is truly remarkable about these letters is their faithful, completely honest reporting of circumstances and events that Frank[10] experienced. Nothing is left out. The letters do indeed tell the whole story of those three years, at least as Frank[10] saw it. Friends who also were in the military and communicated with their parents have unanimously said that their correspondence was far less revealing. There was much that they left unreported and unsaid. They have been impressed that Frank[10] felt sufficiently comfortable to reveal everything he was experiencing and feeling to his mother. There was clearly an openness of communication that does not often exist between generations.

Frank[10] did not keep his mother's correspondence as carefully. He was moving around a great deal, and difficulties were encountered maintaining anything. Further, there were many letters.

She wrote to him every day. There were probably 1000 letters over the three years. The majority were four pages, with about one third V-mail (a single page

---

[61] *Letters from Frank P. Sherwood to His Mother, Mildred P. Sherwood.* (Tallahassee, Florida: personally published, April 24, 2000, 382 pages, plus documents.

that was photographed and reduced in size to reduce the volume of shipping). She engaged in this prodigious letter-writing throughout the war when she was working at her flower shop six days a week from 9 a.m to 9 p.m. Almost all the letters were penned after 9 p.m. at the end of an exhausting 12-hour day.

Frank[10] found he had 100 letters from his mother. He has Xeroxed them and placed them in a book.[62] About two-thirds are of the four page variety and a third V-mails. [Recently he has found more letters which have not yet been organized.] In working on Mildred's letters, Frank[10] came to realize she had the gene that gave him his interest in writing. In his introduction to his mother's volume, he observed that there were four features of her letters that are particularly noteworthy. First, she was *verbal*. She was able to write a lot, though she must have been dead tired. Second, she had a *love of words*. Mildred was regularly trying out new words. Third, she was concerned about reader *interest*. She expressed concern that her prose was not exactly compelling. She had a quantitative target to produce a letter a day, and she found something of interest to report a remarkable percentage of the time. Finally, she had a sense of *humor*. She sought desperately to write something that would raise her son's spirits. It is sad that Frank[10] did not discover some of Mildred's remarkable talents until long after her death.

Mildred at about age 56 with two of our favorite dogs, Pete on left, Teufel on right.

Frank[10] and his mother were living in a house in Pacific Beach when he and Frances Howell decided to get married. Frank[10], of course, wanted the best of all worlds. He sought to stay with his mother and bring another wonderful young woman into the household. This was an arrangement fraught with disaster. That it did not end up that way is a credit to both these great people. Almost everyone would say it was no way to treat a beautiful young wife, i.e. to put her in the same house with her mother-in-law. Mildred undoubtedly started from the premise that no one was good enough for her wonderful boy, but that is not a message she chose to convey to Frances. To her son she always declared her delight with the marriage and with the bride. Both Mildred and Frances worked hard to support each other, and they made things work. Some measure of the problem is seen in a

---

[62] *Wartime Letters from Mildred P. Sherwood to Her Son Frank P. Sherwood.* (Tallahassee, Florida: personally published, July 28, 2000), 273 pages.

comment that Lois Elizabeth James, Frank[10]'s cousin, made to Frances. "I can't tell you how pleased we are with the marriage. We had a tremendous worry that Frank[10] would always be a momma's boy."

The last vignette recreates a scene on the University of Southern California campus in about 1953 when Mildred and Frank[10] encountered a professorial colleague, William Bruce Storm, with whom a close and affectionate relationship has continued over nearly 60 years. After the usual pleasantries, Bruce turned to Mildred and said, "Mrs. Sherwood, there is one thing you have done for Frank[10] that should make you very proud. You have given him tremendous personal confidence." It was really quite an off-handed remark but it was crucially significant. Frank[10] noted it at the time and recognized that Mildred had been highly important in giving him an assuredness and a belief in himself. Later, as he worked with many executives, Frank[10] came to realize how critical self-confidence is in working with others. If you don't believe in yourself, you are not likely to trust others. Mildred had truly given him one of the greatest of gifts.

Mildred Persons Sherwood Dies on November 19, 1978

Mildred Persons Sherwood died just a week short of her 83rd birthday on November 18, 1978, in Charlottesville, Virginia. The last 13 years of her life were not at all happy ones. They were spent in nursing homes, primarily in Charlottesville, Virginia, where her son had moved in August, 1968. At that time she was flown east to be with him. As noted earlier, the details of her later life are reported in Appendix 1, "The Widowhood of Mildred Persons Sherwood."

The 13 years in the nursing homes witnessed a continuing deterioration of her health, both physically and mentally. She was bedridden for a considerable length of time and really had not been ambulatory since 1966. The cause of death was said to be pneumonia, but the reality is that she was only a shell of her former self.

A very small service was held in a mortuary in Charlottesville, led by her son and attended by Frances and Mildred's two grandchildren, Jeffrey[11] and Robin Ann[11]. In Charlottesville her only trips away from the nursing home were to her son's house. She knew no one in Charlottesville.

Mildred was cremated, and the following year Frank[10] and Frances took the ashes to Fort Plain, New York, where they were placed in the grave of her beloved husband.

CHAPTER III

Frank[10] Persons Sherwood, the Tenth Generation

This chapter inaugurates a new dimension in the book. From this point, the reader will find that the principal characters were still alive when these chapters were being written. That situation poses opportunities and problems. The great advantage is that this later family history will be much better informed because the people who lived the events are still around to tell about them. The downside is that some of the objectivity may be lost. Detachment is not possible.

As has been recorded in the previous chapter, Frank[10] was born in Brunswick, Georgia, on October 11, 1920. Thus he recorded his 85th birthday in 2005. As will be considered in much greater detail later in the chapter, he married Frances Howell on February 14, 1948. She was born November 21, 1926 and had her 79th birthday in 2005. The marriage and the infusion of the Howell blood into the Sherwood family tree provides the major thrust of the next chapter; and the chronicle of the family (consisting of the parents and the two offspring) form the content for the succeeding one.

In keeping with the pattern established in the book, this chapter begins with biographical data on Frank[10] Sherwood.

Early Memories of Frank[10] Persons Sherwood

For Frank[10], his life really began in San Diego, California. He has no recollection of his father, Clarence[9], or of life in Brunswick. As far as he was concerned, he grew up the only child of a single mother. And it was the arrival at the house on 25th street, and the enthusiasm of his grandparents and aunt and uncle, that constitute his first memories. His mother, his grandparents, his great grandfather Joseph James, his aunt and uncle Lois and Ross Carter, and his cousin Elizabeth (Pose) were his family.

Brooklyn Elementary School

While the 25th street house represented physical stability in his youth, it was originally only a temporary shelter. Mildred wanted her own home, and so a duplex at 27th and A streets in San Diego became the shelter for the small boy and his mother. The Brooklyn Elementary School on 30th street was only about three long blocks away; and it was there that Frank[10] began academic life in September, 1925. He had not yet turned five, but things were apparently more relaxed in those days. An institution of some age even in 1925, Brooklyn occupied a large city block; and its original building of two stories, which was fairly imposing, stood about in the center and on the eastern (30th street) edge of the property. Later, on the northern and western sides of the block, other buildings had been erected. Classroom assignments followed an hierarchical formula, with students rotating around from the kindergarten facility at the northeastern edge to the center of the building on the western side, then to the two-story structure. The rest of the later building housed administrative offices, a rather substantial library, a cafeteria, and an assembly hall. The facilities were quite generous; and the younger students were in classrooms with outdoor exits.

Yet the old, two story building possessed the real status. Young students looked to the time when they escaped the pleasant, well lit, well-ventilated, outer classrooms and were fifth and sixth graders in the older, less inviting major building.

Because the school system was organized on a half-year basis at that time, with entrance possible both in September and February, two classrooms were allocated for each grade level. The fourth grade, for example, had students in 4a and 4b. The 4a students constituted the older group whose next step would be 5b.

As would be expected, there were two graduations, one in June and the other in February. This arrangement was quite important for Frank[10] because he started out in September and ended graduating in February, half year ahead of the people with whom he began. The reason: he "skipped" in the fourth grade. That meant he moved from 4b (the September group) to 4a (the February group). The advancement gave him much satisfaction. Frank[10] took it to mean that the teachers saw him as a bright guy and able to deal with a higher level of work. But it did bring substantial change. February classes were always smaller and somewhat less significant in the scheme of things. That arrangement persisted through high school, from which he graduated in February 1938.

As it does in 2006, place of residence generally determined the school one would attend. For his first two years at Brooklyn, Frank[10] had no problem. As a five-year-old, he walked the three blocks to school by himself, as did most of his fellow students. No one felt there was much risk; and, anyway, that was what kids did. Few families had two cars; and the best a mother could have done was walk with her child. It just didn't seem necessary. In Frank[10]'s case, his mother was working.

The Brooklyn school years, seven of them, went by quickly; and, except for a generally happy time, Frank remembers relatively little. Very likely the most important piece of Brooklyn School was meeting Edwin Self. They got to know each other in the 4th grade, shortly after Eddie (as he was then known) had arrived from Oshkosh, Wisconsin. They became bosom buddies by the 6th grade, and that persisted for the rest of their lives.[63]

The skip from Grade 4b to 4a (which changed him from a June to February graduate) was, of course, of immediate and long-term importance. Somewhat less significant was the time Frank was selected as one of a few boys and girls to appear in the San Diego High School production of *Little Lord Fauntleroy*. Pictures taken at the time reflect his enthusiasm for donning tails at an early age.

Interestingly, the library and the cafeteria at Brooklyn school were important physical marks of the experience. The library was a substantial operation. It clearly was not an add-on. The cafeteria, too, was in a special part and not used for any other purpose. Frank remembers feeling really good about the food. He sensed that he was eating out, something that did not happen very often in his family.

"Little Lord Fauntleroy". Taken at the San Diego house on 25th street. The Cooper mansion is in the background.

Golden Hill Playground

Any reminiscences about Brooklyn School as a place must be co-mingled with Golden Hill Playground.[64] This great facility, with a substantial clubhouse, six tennis courts, baseball field, and a croquet court, as well as the usual playground

---

[63] See Frank P. Sherwood, *A Twenty Year Journey with Edwin Forbes Self*. Tallahassee, Florida: June, 1996, 25 p. This monograph was written shortly after Ed's death in 1996 and covers the period 1929-1949, when their relationship was particularly close.

[64] See Frank P. Sherwood, *Growing up in the Golden Hill Neighborhood of San Diego, California, 1924-1939*. Tallahassee, Florida: June 7, 2000. This monograph contains considerable detail on the environment in which Frank matured.

facilities, lay about half-way between Frank's[10] house and Brooklyn School. The playground director, Clyde Johnson, was an important figure. He was a great friend. And it was a place where Frank[10] got to know older kids, one of whom, Ambrose Schindler, went on to football stardom. He was an All-American quarterback at the University of Southern California. What Frank[10] particularly remembers about him, though, was his high jumping ability.

Though the playground sat at the very edge of Balboa Park, an indelible recollection is that everything was dirt. There was not a blade of grass to be found in the whole expanse. Furthermore, the nine-hole municipal golf course, just to the north of Golden Hill Playground, was also entirely dirt, even the greens. They were called greens, but of course they weren't. There were likely two reasons for the presence of so much dirt. First, it was a big burden to mow grass, which had to be performed entirely by hand-pushed reel mowers of very limited width. They never seemed to be adjusted and to make an acceptable cut. A new, larger grass course replaced the dirt one in the middle 30s; and one of the great marvels was the gas-powered, ride mower that manicured the fairways. The second problem was water. We didn't have much of it, and that problem persisted until San Diego was able to import Colorado River water.

Roosevelt Junior High School

The move to the 7th grade and Roosevelt Junior High School in January, 1932, was exciting but traumatic. It meant moving to a location much further away that enrolled kids from a larger geographical area. In point of fact, though, the differences were probably more psychological than real. Frank continued to be out of district by about two blocks; but the streetcar transportation was so remarkable that it took less time to get to Roosevelt than to walk to Brooklyn. The streetcar ran within two blocks of Frank's house at 25th and Broadway and then descended from that point to 12th and Broadway, less than a 10 minute ride. A transfer put Frank[10] on another trolley that went north through Balboa Park and stopped about a block from Roosevelt. The total trip was less than 20 minutes, and the streetcars ran with great frequency. Also, there was virtually no cost. A pass to use the trolleys on all school days was $1 per month.

Somehow, though, it seemed to Frank that he had crossed a great divide on entering Roosevelt. He was going through puberty, and a disgusting outbreak of acne, which would plague him for the next six years, was beginning to appear. Moreover, he had become aware of body odor. Up to that time, he had worn his clothes for several days (there being no washing machine at his house) with no great problems. He had to find new ways to keep himself presentable and odorless at the very time he was beginning to discover there were girls in the world. On top of these major problems of personal transformation, the organization of the classes at Roosevelt Junior

High School was dramatically different. There was no one teacher who would see you all day and with whom you would develop a strong bond; instead, you now shuttled between classes, with time always at a premium. The transition from elementary to junior high school has always seemed to Frank far more daunting than the later moves to high school and to college.

Growing Friendship with Eddie Self

At Roosevelt the friendship with Eddie Self was even more significant. By that time the two boys had become interested in newspapers, though Eddie's concerns were more pronouncedly with the comics. He had the great hope that he would become a cartoonist and spent much time drawing. Frank[10] thought Eddie's stuff was very good and envied the fact that he might have a career possibility. Roosevelt had a school newspaper that appeared a number of times a year and was hand set and produced in its print shop. Eddie and Frank[10] both worked on the paper, and Frank[10] somehow became the editor of the *Rough Rider*, the appropriate name for the newspaper of a school identified with Theodore Roosevelt.

Wilbur Folsom and First Tennis

When Frank was in the eighth grade, a man with an artificial leg and a bad limp showed up at Roosevelt to complete his practice teaching requirement. Before he lost his leg Wilbur Folsom had been an avid tennis player, and his enthusiasm did not decline because he had great difficulty moving on the court. He essentially hopped on one foot. To provide some outlet for his tennis enthusiasms, he personally launched and coached a school tennis team. Frank[10] found Folsom quite wonderful and felt he learned a lot from him. The relationship might have been a great deal closer, but Wilbur Folsom could not accept, and only tolerated, Frank[10]'s temper tantrums on the tennis court. When his practice teaching year was concluded, Folsom could find no job and opened a tennis shop near a municipal tennis facility. Though he felt he had learned a lot from Folsom, Frank[10] was so disgusted with himself that he played relatively little tennis when he was in high school. Though always pleasant, the visits to the Folsom tennis shop were relatively infrequent.

Once the problem of body odor was handled, girls became an increasing presence in junior high school life. When Frank[10] was in the eighth grade, he went to the Townsend school of dance; and, in the ninth, he attended his first "semi-formal" dance. What made the occasion semi-formal was that the girls were fully formal and the boys were in dark suits, no tuxedos. A particularly pleasant memory was of "penny noon" dances at Roosevelt, which were held each Friday in the school courtyard. Just about everyone showed up, and the charge was just what the name suggested, a penny a dance.

Two Special Teachers

There were two teachers at Roosevelt with a particular presence in Frank's memory. One was his Latin teacher, Ida Parker, who was very close to retirement. She was a delightful old woman who loved Latin and was able to impart that enthusiasm to her first year students. Each year the class members, dressed in togas, performed a play in Latin for the entire student body. Only Mrs. Parker's excitement for the project could give legs to a play performed in a dead language.

The other unforgettable individual was Leah Colbert. She was the home room teacher, an assignment she held throughout Frank[10]'s three years at Roosevelt. The idea of the home room was to give students an anchor point, an island of stability, but it does not appear that this concept has survived the many reforms in education. What made Miss Colbert special was that she had had Frank[10]'s mother, Mildred, at the Florence elementary school years before.

San Diego High School

The move to San Diego High School in January, 1935, was unremarkable. Structurally, the education process was much the same. One obvious difference, though, was that San Diego High was about three times larger, enrolling about 3000 students. It was by far the largest educational institution in the city at that time. And it was a far more diverse community. Beyond that, San Diego High was replete with a tradition that its buildings symbolized.[65] It was known as the "Gray Castle," which was exactly how it looked. Its venerability was further emphasized by the ivy that clung to its walls. It really was an "ivied" institution. San Diego was then a young community

The main building of San Diego High School. To the right (outside the picture) was the Russ Auditorium, then the major performing arts center in the city; and to the left was another major building, also covered in ivy. The sign, SDHS, at the top between the two turrets, was the result of a campaign which Frank led.

and so SDHS was perceived as really old, having been established about 40 years

---

[65] It is important to report that Frances Howell. the future spouse, is also a graduate of San Diego High School (June, 1944) and shared the feeling that it was a great place.

earlier. Yet, surprisingly, the Castle stood on a hill close to downtown San Diego without identification. Apparently no one felt it necessary to state specifically what the Castle was. Frank[10] rectified that situation. He organized a committee to raise money, with the result that the needed $250 was secured and a school sign, sdhs in old English letters, was erected over the main entrance.

Outstanding Faculty

The professional staff at San Diego High was truly incredible. As Frank[10] observed years later, these were people who belonged in higher education. The principal, John Aseltine, was particularly special. He was always accessible, always interested, and was a clear presence in the system without being controlling. He was a masterful executive. Perhaps because of his attractiveness, he had assembled a unique faculty and given them license to shape a curriculum that was in touch with the needs of those very tough economic times. This was particularly true in the social sciences. Frank[10] remembers taking courses in Democracy, the New Deal, and Local Government with really outstanding teachers. He was exposed to the realities of World War I, and the general argument that it had been a massive mistake. There is no doubt that Frank[10] left San Diego High with the strong conviction that war is the worst possible means of resolving conflict in the world.

The strength of the school was not just in the social sciences. Run through nearly everything that is important in culture and you would find it at San Diego High School, with highly effective teachers in drama, symphony, glee club, debate, language, and athletics.

The Russ School Newspaper: Consuming Interest and Superb Development Vehicle

The school newspaper, *The Russ*, held a particularly special place in this galaxy of the exciting undertakings beyond the classroom. The pivot of it all was Verl Freyburger Smurthwaite, the adviser. She had for years invested herself completely in the paper, living in an apartment just about a block from the school. The small room that housed *The Russ* office was Frank[10]'s home for his three years in high school. It had a small alcove at the end of the room where Mrs. Smurthwaite sat. Long tables with typewriters, formed in a U, occupied virtually all the remaining space. There could be no mistake that Mrs. Smurthwaite was at the center. The scene replicated a newspaper office, with all the energy (between 3 p.m. and 7 p.m.) of a reportorial staff facing a deadline.

Ed and Frank[10] were a part of that *Russ* scene almost before they knew what classes they were taking at San Diego High. And so it continued for three years. The busiest time was on Monday when most of the articles had to be written and submitted to the student editors and Mrs. Smurthwaite. Tuesday was for editing and rewriting, which was a continuous process. As stories were completed and approved, they were transported to the School's print shop, where *The Russ* retained a full time printer who operated the linotype and got the type ready for printing. On Thursday the paper was printed; and it was distributed Friday mornings. There was always a buzz when *The Russ* came out because it was the only real means of communication in a community of more than 3000 students and faculty. [66]

Ed was named editor of *The Russ* in his Senior B year and then was elected President of his class in the Senior A year. [Remember, we graduated in January.] Frank[10] was editor in his Senior A year, after having served as Student Body Vice President in his Senior B year. An article by Ed had brought him the national high school newspaper writing top award [and a portable typewriter] in his junior year and Frank[10] gained the same recognition and typewriter as a senior.

By the time he assumed the editorship, Frank[10] was fairly well convinced that his future lay in newspaper publishing. The news side was the most important, of course, but he wanted to get as much experience of the whole of the newspaper enterprise as he could. As a result, he also assumed the position of *Russ* advertising manager, for which, incidentally, there were no other candidates. *The Russ* was converted into a tabloid, which was regarded as a tremendous break with tradition; and the presswork was transferred from the high school print shop to a downtown San Diego publisher. That avoided a lot of grief because the old high school press was consistently breaking down. But it meant that costs went up. The subscription price rose from 25 cents per semester to 35, without a loss of circulation. About 2200 of the 3000 students in the school paid their 35 cents, not an insignificant amount in those days.

Tom Ludwig Makes the Ed and Frank[10] Relationship a Triumverate

While Ed and Frank[10] retained their close relationship, they embraced a third person, Thomas Ludwig. He appeared in San Diego High School in the sophomore year and was a person of great intelligence, wit, and charm. He was most emphatically not middle class. His family had migrated from Arkansas; and it took everything, including welfare, for them to survive. This was a time of deep depres-

---

[66] See Frank P. Sherwood, *The Russ in Its 40th Year: The San Diego High School Newspaper Sixty Years Ago*. No place, October, 1998. This monograph was written at the time *The Russ* celebrated its 100th anniversary. The purpose was to show how the newspaper was operating 60 years earlier.

sion, and labeling someone an "Okie" or an "Arkie" was highly demeaning. Yet Tom had no problem with such image issues. Undoubtedly he was the most influential and best liked person in the class. Among other things, his column in *The Russ*, which typically combined humor and gossip, was undoubtedly the best read piece of the paper. Not surprisingly, Tom was elected student body president.

There is one other person who was a major figure in Frank's high school experience. Her name then was Dorothy McCloskey. At Roosevelt Junior High, she was the first girl Frank[10] dated. (It was for that semi-formal dance.) When she and Ed reached high school, they became a duo that persisted through high school and college, ending in marriage in 1943. The two best friends in some respects shared a girl but not romantically. Dorothy, too, was an important actor at *The Russ*. She was the assistant editor in her Senior A year and was also vice president of the student body at the same time.

Graduation at San Diego High was highlighted in those days by the bestowal of a "Citizenship Trophy" on the outstanding boy and outstanding girl in the class. There

From left, Frank[10], Ed Self, and Tom Ludwig holding the Citizenship Trophy.

was no question about the female recipient. It was Dorothy McCloskey, and the expectation was that Tom Ludwig would be recognized as the top boy. The great surprise was that the committee (composed of students and faculty) did something that had never been done before.[67] The trophy was awarded to three people, Tom, Ed, and Frank[10]. It is possible that the three boys felt this was the best possible outcome, at least Frank[10] did.

Grade Success

Frank[10] has no record of his grades at San Diego High, but they were undoubtedly very good. He and Ed consistently competed, with the implicit ground rule that they were to stay even with each other. Anything less than an A was unacceptable, as far as both were concerned.

The program for the class commencement on January 28, 1938 shows that 19 students [out of 240] made the class Honor Roll, whose standard was at least 11

---

[67] It was recorded in *The Russ* that the trophy had been given to two boys in 1931.

A's in the first five semesters at San Diego High. Tom, Ed, and Frank[10] were in this group. The California Scholarship Federation, a statewide organization with a substantial presence at San Diego High, awarded life memberships to 15 students with gold seals placed on their diplomas. The standard was presence on the class honor roll at least two-thirds of the time in school. Tom, Ed, and Frank[10] were among the five boys [with 10 girls] receiving CSF life memberships.

Though the history books declare that the economy had improved in 1938 from the 1933 bottom, most people found the improvements very difficult to detect. There were no jobs for young high school graduates. Indeed, it did not seem as if there were <u>any</u> jobs. Further, there was little that promised improvement in the future. The questions for the young man were how to survive, not a search for an opportunity that would promise challenge and fulfillment. [At that time career prospects for females very much centered on marriage, teaching, nursing, and librarianship.] It was a time, of course, when relatively few high school graduates, even from an institution as well regarded as San Diego High, went on to college. While Frank[10] stated in the school yearbook that he planned to matriculate at Pomona, it was a very remote expectation.

In such an environment, hopes and expectations were minimal; and additional education did not seem to make much difference. Frank[10]'s uncle, Ross S. Carter, with an MD degree from the prestigious Johns Hopkins University and a bachelor's from Stanford, was just barely getting by. Frank[10] specifically remembers the financial target for his best years, $200 per month, $2400 a year. That was a little less than the salary of a senior teacher at San Diego High with about 20 years of experience.

Time off from School: The Trip East and Working at The San Diego Sun

It seemed better to move into the real world and secure at least a modest foothold in the struggle to make out in life. Further, Frank[10] faced a financial problem. His mother had no money to send him away to school. At the moment only San Diego State College was a possibility. There was a source of funds, however, that would become available to him. Frank[8] Sherwood, his grandfather, had died on January 16, 1938, and left him half his estate. But the will had to be probated, a time-consuming process. The inheritance, between $15,000 and $20,000 [records of the exact amount have been lost], was substantial, given the value of money at that time. Frank[10] was not at all certain how he wanted to use the money; but a decision was not immediately required. It would not be available in time to go to school in the fall.

Trip to New York and Washington, D.C.

Not long after Frank[10]'s graduation, a truly marvelous thing happened. The Columbia Scholastic Press Association, housed at Columbia University in New York City, contacted *The Russ* adviser, Verl Smurthwaite, and asked her to nominate a person to be the California representative at the Association's annual convention. Miraculously, the money was found for the trip, and Frank[10], as the most recent editor, was named the representative. He departed on March 7, 1938, heading first for New York City and the convention and then on to Washington, D.C., where he had the great fortune of attending one of President Franklin D. Roosevelt's press conferences.[68]

Classified Advertising Salesman

Back in San Diego after the heady experience in the east, Frank[10] began an earnest search for a job. The editorial departments of the newspapers in town yielded nothing, but the classified advertising manager at the town's third newspaper, the *San Diego Sun*, took an interest in him. Harvey Hall, who had a drinking problem, was a courtly man, a graduate of Grinnell College, and an all-around nice person. Frank could not have found a better boss. The pay, of course, was nothing about which to brag, 25 cents a hour, eight hours a day, six days a week. The grand total was $12 per week, exactly what Ed Self was making in a book store.

But the work was demoralizing. It involved selling classified advertising outside the San Diego downtown, mostly to businesses; but if there were a "For Rent" sign on a house, it also required a call. What was discouraging was that an advertisement in *The Sun* generated virtually no responses. Few people, including small businesses, had money to waste. So Frank[10] felt himself peddling a worth-

---

[68] See *Letters from Frank P. Sherwood to his Mother Mildred P. Sherwood, 1931-1943*. Reston, Virginia: 2004, pgs. 4-8. See also Appendix I which describes Frank[10]'s attendance at President Roosevelt's press conference.

less product. He was not successful, either because he was not a very good salesman or because he did not believe in what he was doing.

The one person who gave him encouragement was Harvey Hall, who kept insisting that *The Sun* and its advertisements were high quality. Then Harvey Hall suddenly died, about four months after Frank[10] had begun work. Within two weeks Hall's successor had fired Frank[10]. By summer Frank[10] was out of a job. A little later he was hired as editor of a small neighborhood newspaper, the *East San Diego Press,* where he worked for about six months for the princely sum of $5 per week. It was his estimate that the publisher and owner of the paper was making very little more.

Planning for College

During this period Frank[10] was worrying about his future. He had taken the College Boards, had done well on them, and really had his pick of colleges. His greatest disappointment was that he had not received the William Pierce Johnson Fellowship from Dartmouth College, reserved for a Californian. That generous scholarship had made it possible for Ed Self to go to Dartmouth in the fall of 1938. For Frank[10] his inheritance proved to be something of a problem. When he had visited Columbia University, he had said that he would not touch his inheritance to go to school. The Columbia people accepted that point of view and were optimistic that there were ways for Frank[10] to make ends meet there. He followed the same philosophy in the Dartmouth scholarship application, not mentioning the inheritance. The conclusion at Dartmouth was that, even with the scholarship, he did not have the means to support himself. Hence the award went to someone else.

Despite the positive response at Columbia, it was reasonably clear that Frank[10] would have to pay his way at any of the other good private colleges. The University of California at Berkeley was the only highly reputable institution he could attend without a substantial personal expenditure. It really came down to Dartmouth or Berkeley. Ed Self's enthusiasm for Dartmouth won the day, even though Frank[10] had real misgivings about making such a major draw on his inheritance.

Dartmouth College

The Dartmouth years, 1939-1942, were spent entirely in a wartime environment. World War II commenced with Hitler's invasion of Poland shortly after Frank[10] arrived in Hanover. The fall of France in the spring of 1940 was all anyone thought about on the campus. Then, Pearl Harbor occurred roughly two years later. Frank[10] still remembers casually going to the reserve desk in Baker Library on the night of December 7, 1941, and there finding a handwritten note, "The Japs have bombed Pearl Harbor." The shock will never be forgotten.

Although a war does not provide the best setting for college life, it has to be admitted that life was in many ways pleasant, often eventful, and generally rewarding. The best way to get a feel for these times is to read Frank[10]'s letters to his mother.[69] Aside from the overhang of the war, the expense of going to Dartmouth constituted a persistent worry. Though he had a small advertising business that yielded him a relatively good income, Frank[10] found that the College was making a substantial claim on his inheritance. Of greater concern, however, was the tremendous chasm between his life style and that of his mother. While he felt guilty much of the time, he did want to partake fully of the world in which he found himself. That required money.

Frank Joins Ed Self at Dartmouth

Overall, Dartmouth afforded Frank[10] a wonderful education experience. Classes were small and on the whole challenging, access to professors was easy and the associations enriching, and so there was much that made him feel he was investing his time and money well. The relationship with his dear friend, Ed Self, continued to be stimulating and rewarding. The two were highly competitive with each other, and the relationship provided much of the stimulus for better grades. There was one semester when both got straight A's. Frank[10]'s Dartmouth transcript, which is summarized on the next page, shows he ranked fourth of 488 men graduating. His grade point average for classes taken at Dartmouth was 3.77.

It cannot be said that Frank[10] was a significant person in the class. One reason for the high degree of anonymity was that he wanted nothing to get in the way of doing as well as possible in his studies. He was a "grind." The second reason was that the College, with 3,000 energetic and generally ambitious boys, had evolved into a highly specialized system. You didn't dabble with the college newspaper, for example. You had to give it all your free time in order to achieve any status on it. Ed chose a different route and competed to become a manager of one of the College's athletic teams. It's a wonder he did so well academically because he spent a major amount of time moving up a very hierarchical ladder of sports team management. In the end he got the top job, the student manager for the whole athletic operation, with substantial perks, but he gave up a lot to get there.

---

[69] *Letters from Frank Sherwood to his Mother Mildred P. Sherwood, 1931-43, loc. cit.*

Frank[10]'s standing in the class was somewhat compromised because he left Dartmouth in the spring semester, 1942, to return to San Diego to be with his mother, who had suffered a nervous breakdown. It was a time when people on the West Coast really feared a Japanese invasion. As a result, Frank[10] did not feel

---

ACADEMIC RECORD AT DARTMOUTH
(The Transcript is not provided here because it did not produce well.)

1st Semester 1939-40		1st Semester 1940-41		1st Semester 1941-42		1st Semester Summer-42	
Classic Civ.	A	Botany 1	A	Econ. Geophy	C	Physics 1-2	A-A
English	A	Economics	A	Pol. Sci. 17	A	Pol. Sci. 18	A
French	A	English 19	A	Pol. Sci. 51	A	Pol. Sci. 101	A
Geology	A	French 53	A	Pol. Sci. honors	A	Pol. Sci. Honors	B
Social Science	A	Pol. Sci. 1	A	Psychology 1	B	2nd Semester Fall 42	
2nd Semester 1939-40		2nd Semester 1940-41		2nd Semester - SD State		Accounting	A
Classic Civ.	A	English 20	B	Speech	A	Mathematics	B
English	A	French 54	B	English	A	Pol. Sci. 13	A
French 2	A	Pol. Sci. 12	A	Pol. Sci.	B	Pol. Sci. 102	A
Geology	B	Sociology 1	A	War Econ	B	Pol. Sci. Honors	A
Social Science	A	Zoology 1	A	Mod. Econ Thot	A		

---

comfortable in Hanover. Back in San Diego, he took a full load at San Diego State College. But there was a problem. While Dartmouth transferred credit for the courses taken, there was no recognition of grades. Consequently, Frank[10] did not become a member of Phi Beta Kappa and he was not given special recognition on his diploma, such as Summa Cum Laude.

Class of 1926 Fellowship

The most significant award Frank[10] received from Dartmouth was the Class of 1926 Fellowship. It provided sufficient funds for a semester of graduate work. At the beginning of 1943, military service (and the draft into the Army) seemed the only option. He was in no doubt, of course, about his relatively immediate future. Frank[10] had to go to war, even though he was not enthused with the prospect. However, he decided to see if he could tease out another semester before beginning his military service. The National Institute of Public Affairs in Washington, D.C. was a highly interesting possibility. He was admitted but had the problem of convincing his draft board in San Diego that it merited a deferment. Fortunately, the population of potential draftees was very large at that time, and also a member of the National Institute board was the Secretary of War, Henry L. Stimson. The Institute letter proposing a deferment, with the Stimson name on the letterhead, may have been persuasive in the draft board's decision to grant a deferment. The roughly four months in Washington provided an extremely exciting time and are described in some detail in Frank[10]'s letters to his mother.[70]

Three Years of Service in the U.S. Army

In September, 1943, Frank[10] reported for the draft in San Diego. A full account of his experience in the Army may be found in a 381 page volume of all the letters he wrote to his mother.[71] On pages 74 and 75, Frank[10]'s Separation Record is reproduced. It is the official summation of his three years of military service.

Another way of summarizing the military experience of Frank[10] is the Table of Contents of the *Letters* volume. Since the letters were organized on a chronological basis, the Table provides a sequential view of the three years, starting with basic training at Camp Wolters, Texas, moving ultimately to the European theater as an infantry lieutenant, and concluding as a Public Safety officer in Military Government.

I. **BASIC TRAINING AT CAMP WOLTERS, TEXAS SEPT. 24, 1943-MARCH 29, 1944**
Formal training ended Jan. 31, 1944, but it was March 31, 1944, before I left Camp Wolters.
Section covers letters dated Sept. 24, 1943 to March 29, 1944

II. **WITH THE 10TH MOUNTAIN DIVISION APRIL 3, 1944-JULY 15, 1944**
First at Camp Hale, Colorado, April 3, 1944, then to Camp Swift, Texas, June 24, 1944, departing July 25, 1944
Section covers letters dated April 3, 1944 to July 23, 1944

2nd Lieutenant
Frank Sherwood

---

[70] *Letters from Frank Sherwood to his Mother Mildred P. Sherwood, 1931-43*, loc. cit.
[71] *One World War II Experience: Letters from Frank P. Sherwood to his Mother Mildred P. Sherwood, Covering Three Years in the U.S. Army with Ranks from Buck Private to First Lieutenant, September 24, 1943 to September 10, 1946*. Tallahassee, FL: April. 2000, xeroxed, 381 p.

III. **OFFICERS CANDIDATE SCHOOL-FORT BENNING, GEORGIA JULY 25, 1944-NOVEMBER 18, 1944**
16 Weeks of Arduous Challenges in order to Become an Expendable Second Lieutenant of Infantry
Section covers letters dated July 25, 1944 to November 18, 1944

IV. **FIRST MONTHS AS AN OFFICER AND QUICKLY SHIPPING OVERSEAS DECEMBER 11, 1944-FEBRUARY 20, 1944**
A Brief Stint at Camp Hood, Texas-Shipment to Europe-Waiting in a Replacement Depot. Section covers letters dated December 11, 1944 to February 13, 1945

V. **COMBAT WITH THE 99TH INFANTRY DIVISION FEBRUARY 20, 1945-JULY 10, 1945**
Liaison Control Officer in Division's Forward Command Post during War, in the Special Services Division after hostilities ended.
Section covers letters dated February 20, 1945 to July 8, 1945

VI. **ENTERTAINMENT OFFICER, XV CORPS JULY 10, 1945-OCTOBER 13, 1945**
There were 200,000 troops in XV Corps, and I had to see they were entertained with movies and visiting stars from the U.S. I got a real break when I was temporarily reassigned to study at Oxford University.
Section covers letters dated July 10, 1945 to October 12, 1945

VII. **THE TWO MONTH INTERLUDE AT OXFORD UNIVERSITY OCTOBER 13, 1945-DECEMBER 16, 1945**
Oxford was my peak experience in the Army. What a break! I was one of about 40 in the European Theater who were lucky enough to go to Oxford.
Section covers letters dated October 13, 1945 to December 20, 1945

VIII. **BACK IN GERMANY WITH XV CORPS ENTERTAINMENT DECEMBER 23, 1945-MARCH 6, 1946**
It was a letdown to return to Bamberg, Germany, and to a Corps rapidly being dismantled.
Section covers letters dated December 23, 1945 to March 5, 1946

IX. **MILITARY GOVERNMENT MARCH 6, 1946-AUGUST 20, 1946**
Public Safety Officer in three local MG detachments: Naila, Kulmbach, Stadt Steinach
Section covers letters dated March 6, 1946 to August 15, 1946

X. **TO BREMERHAVEN AND HOME AUGUST 20, 1946-SEPTEMBER 10, 1946**
A big piece of this action was taking my dog, Gus, with me.
Section covers letters dated August 20, 1946 to September 18, 1946

Operating a Small Newspaper with Ed Self

Within about a week after returning to San Diego in September, 1946, Frank[10] and Ed Self departed on a newspaper-hunting tour that took them as far north as the State of Washington. Frank[10] has always regarded the experience of working with Ed Self in publishing a newspaper one of the major features of his life. It therefore deserves reasonably full coverage in this chapter. An excerpt from a volume Frank[10] wrote at the time of Ed's death provides a reasonable summary of the period.[72]

> When we returned to San Diego and found that we could buy the paper in the suburb of Pacific Beach, just south of La Jolla, it was a go. The price seemed rich, $20,000, but we could swing it; and we paid all cash, about half of it provided by my mother. We of course knew the territory. Pacific Beach was a high growth area, which met one of our criteria. The *North Shores Sentinel* was a typical small town paper, with a paid circulation of about 600 and clearly with no pretense of editorial quality or marketing savvy. We figured we ought to be able to do something with it. The equipment was very old, including one linotype of early vintage. One didn't have to be very smart to know that it was going to be a strain to produce a newspaper in this plant. The problem was further compounded by our decision that we had to move from paid to controlled circulation. Under this plan we had to circulate copies to every home in Pacific Beach, about 5,000, and hope that delivery boys could collect a quarter from enough people each month to make their efforts worthwhile. It was an approach that had worked excellently in Los Angeles.
>
> When we were engaged in negotiations with the *Sentinel* publisher, Paul Baker, we noticed that he had cot in his office. It seemed strange and out of place. Very shortly after we took over the operation, we knew exactly why the cot was there. That was where he got 2-3 hours sleep when he was struggling to get out the paper on Wednesday and Thursday nights. Undoubtedly we should have paid more attention to the equipment; but our theory was that we could do anything he could. We also had our eye on the main chance. Pacific Beach did have the capacity to grow; that could mean more revenue and increased goodwill. So we were not entirely crazy.

---

[72] Frank Sherwood, *A Twenty Year Journey with Edwin Forbes Self*. Tallahassee, FL: June, 1996, xeroxed, p. 19-21.

It did not take us long to realize this was not the place for us. However, our partnership was the best part of the whole thing. We got along wonderfully, and I do not recall any real argument between us. We had matured to the point that there was not even the thought of competition. We were in the thing totally together.

It [from p. 73] was a real collaboration. Insofar as the newspaper is concerned, there is no Ed story and Frank story. We were so linked that there were no individual experiences. I do not think I realized it fully at the time, but holding up his end of the bargain was very much tougher on Ed than on me. He had a wife and a child; and there were limits on how much he could absent himself from them. Money was also more important to him. I lived with my mother and needed very little. I am sure it is not the way Ed would have liked to have spent his first years as a father.

Even in the best of circumstances, the workload was extreme. Sundays were usually off; but it was six full days and three nights to the wee hours. The schedule went something like this: Monday—sell advertising; Tuesday—write the paper; Wednesday—work on the composition of the paper, typically doing the dirty work that we did not want to pay our two union compositors to do; Thursday—print 5000 copies of the paper on an old flat bed, involving 20,000 impressions, and also feeding the sheets through an old folder; Friday—deliver the paper (there were always some kids who did not show up); and Saturday—try to collect from our advertisers and do all the detail work of running the organization. In effect, we were drudges. It would be difficult to find anything creative or stimulating in what we were doing. What kept us going, I am sure, was that we did not plan to stay more than three years.

The problems, however, were not ones alone of hard labor. We simply did not like the life and values of the small community, though Pacific Beach was likely no different from thousands of others. Probably most upsetting was the bigotry and narrowness of small business people at that time, 1946-48. I have no idea whether things have changed because I have had no interest at all in any further contact with such people. It was a particular Monday morning problem because that was when we began selling advertising. No matter the prejudice exhibited, we had to keep our mouths shut. It was simply not a world in which two idealistic people had a chance to be authentic.

THE SEPARATION QUALIFICATION RECORD Data on the Front and the Back
BACK OF THE SEPARATION QUALIFICATION RECORD
In this case, the Army did save some paper.

Army of the United States

SEPARATION QUALIFICATION RECORD
SAVE THIS FORM. IT WILL NOT BE REPLACED IF LOST

This record of job assignments and special training received in the Army is furnished to the soldier when he leaves the service. In its preparation, information is taken from available Army records and supplemented by personal interview. The information about civilian education and work experience is based on the individual's own statements. The veteran may present this document to former employers, prospective employers, representatives of schools or colleges, or use it in any other way that may prove beneficial to him.

1. LAST NAME—FIRST NAME—MIDDLE INITIAL				MILITARY OCCUPATIONAL ASSIGNMENTS		
SHERWOOD FRANK P				10. MONTHS	11. GRADE	12. MILITARY OCCUPATIONAL SPECIALTY
2. ARMY SERIAL NO.	3. GRADE	4. SOCIAL SECURITY NO.		6	2nd LT	Public Safety Officer 9000
01328063	1st LT	Unknown				
5. PERMANENT MAILING ADDRESS				4	2nd LT	Liaison Officer Combat 1930
739 25 St San Diego California San Diego Co.						
6. DATE OF ENTRY INTO ACTIVE SERVICE	7. DATE OF SEPARATION	8. DATE OF BIRTH		6	2nd LT	Special Service Officer 5000
28 Nov 44	19 Oct 46	11 Oct 20				
9. PLACE OF SEPARATION						
Separation Center Ft Dix NJ						

SUMMARY OF MILITARY OCCUPATIONS
13. TITLE—DESCRIPTION—RELATED CIVILIAN OCCUPATION

PUBLIC SAFETY OFFICER: Was responsible for Military Government Security in Kreis Naila, and later in Kreis Kulmbach, Bavaria. This position had two Major responsibilities. (A) Supervision of civilian law enforcement by use of civilian police and prisons, close liaison and cooperation with military police and tactical units was also an important responsibility. (B) Denazification of German industry and political life. This involved the establishment of a clerical staff of seven people and the promulgation of procedures to screen civilian questionnaires. A third duty was participation in the operation of military government courts. The public safety officer served as public prosecutor and played an active role in Judicial Determination.

MILITARY EDUCATION

14. NAME OR TYPE OF SCHOOL—COURSE OR CURRICULUM—DURATION—DESCRIPTION

The Infantry School Ft Benning, Ga OCS 17 weeks 1944

CIVILIAN EDUCATION

15. HIGHEST GRADE COMPLETED	16. DEGREES OR DIPLOMAS	17. YEAR LEFT SCHOOL	OTHER TRAINING OR SCHOOLING	
4 yrs College	AB	1942	20. COURSE—NAME AND ADDRESS OF SCHOOL—DATE	21. DURATION
18. NAME AND ADDRESS OF LAST SCHOOL ATTENDED			None	
Dartmouth College, Hanover, NH				
19. MAJOR COURSES OF STUDY				
Political Science				

CIVILIAN OCCUPATIONS

22. TITLE—NAME AND ADDRESS OF EMPLOYER—INCLUSIVE DATES—DESCRIPTION

Student College

ADDITIONAL INFORMATION

23. REMARKS EM 14 Sept 1943 to 27 Nov 1944; Cpl. message Center, infantry OCS 17 weeks. AWARDS: American Campaign Medal, European African Middle Eastern Campaign Medal, with 2 bronze stars; World War 11 Victory Medal, Army of Occupation Medal (Germany)

24. SIGNATURE OF PERSON BEING SEPARATED

Frank P Sherwood

25. SIGNATURE OF SEPARATION CLASSIFICATION OFFICER

J. P. Finley

26. NAME OF OFFICER (Typed or Stamped)

J P FINLEY CAPT AC

...it also has to be admitted that we were encountering stormy financial weather. Partly it was because we had increased revenues; and we were learning we had left out an important variable. The bigger the revenues, the more operating capital is required. We had no till we could tap. Things might not have gotten so bad had we been able to collect our bills promptly. But that is apparently not the nature of the newspaper business—-another variable we had not processed into our calculations. I think we could have sweated things out, but it was not going to be easy.

The *North Shores Sentinel* was sold 18 months later, early in 1948. The details will be discussed in the next chapter.

Marriage!

The time of the *Sentinel* newspaper is highly important for another reason. It was the venue in which Frances Howell and Frank[10] met and began a loving relationship that had continued over 58 years at the time of their anniversary on February 14, 2006. Just how that occurred is described in an excerpt from an unfinished autobiography begun by Frank[10] in 2000.[73]

> A wonderful thing happened when Susie [Her formal name is Frances but Frank[10] never called her that and did not in the autobiography.] came into my life. But things did not start out smoothly. A significant conversation occurred on a Monday evening when Ed and I got back from our advertising rounds. This was always a depressing time, partly because of the bigotry throughout the day we had to experience and also because we never seemed to sell as much advertising as we wanted and needed for true prosperity. On that night, however, Ed was full of pep. He said, "Frank, I have found just the girl for you. She is very attractive, very nice, and she dresses like an Eastern girl."[The Eastern girl was Susie, Frances Howell.]
>
> I think I more or less snorted, "Who has time for girls?" I dismissed Ed's matchmaking effort without further comment. But I did remember he said she

---

[73] Frank P. Sherwood, unfinished autobiography, pages 65-67 in draft.

dressed like an Eastern girl. Unlike the average female in Pacific Beach who thought casual was the only way to go, Ed's nominee dressed in a nice sweater, or perhaps blouse and cardigan, a nicely tailored, conservative skirt, and saddle shoes. That was the common uniform in the eastern colleges but it was all too rare in places like Pacific Beach. So I did understand that Ed was telling me about a special female, even though I just did not feel I had the time for dating. While Ed suggested a particular physical image to me, what was important was the person in the attire. I thought of a compellingly attractive person with a becoming modesty, a conservative style, and a person who radiates quality.

Ed did not push me on the matter; but, a couple of weeks later, he announced to me that he had hired the young woman with the eastern look to work for us on Saturdays, primarily in an editorial capacity. I have to confess I was taken aback by the announcement. Any hiring in our small organization was a fairly major event; and we had always done everything collaboratively. Though put off by his unilateral action, I did agree that we could use the help. And I knew he had good judgement. So I simply said okay. What Susie and I have both concluded is that Ed was determined to be a matchmaker. It wasn't that he was unilateral but rather that he wanted to get us together. We have often agreed that we owe Ed a great debt.

When I saw Susie in our office, I agreed with Ed's appraisal. She was attractive, softly confident, and visibly intelligent. We did not have much to say to each other. All I knew was what I saw. Even though I continued to feel I had no time for women, attractive or not, I did find myself asking her if she would like to have lunch with me on a Saturday or two later. The physical situation is very important in describing this first real encounter between us. We had two desks in a fairly small room with each of them facing an opposite wall. So we were back to back. I turned around to issue the invitation to her. She never even looked at me. She stared at the wall, saying emphatically, "No." The firmness of the refusal came as a surprise to me. I was, after all, one of her bosses; and I was making no great move on her. This was an innocuous suggestion that we go have a bite to eat. My feeling at the time was that this was the end of things. She was clear about her feelings, and mine were not that positive.

Despite the negativity of the situation, it must be concluded that I was drawn to her. In a couple of weeks, I was back asking her to go out with me. This time I got a dramatically different reception. She was quite positive in accepting. Later I learned the reason for the big change. After our initial encounter she had spoken to our staff member, Ruth Hurless, noting that I had invited her to lunch. "I refused him, of course," she recalled saying, "because I did not want to go out with a married man." Ruth's rejoinder was, "Are you crazy? He's not married. He's the most eligible bachelor in town. Why do you think that girl who works at Allison-McCloskey comes in here all the time. I took Susie far to the other side of San Diego, to the La Mesa Inn. I do remember that I had been there a couple of times in the past and thought it was rather pleasant. But I also have a suspicion that I did not want to hang around Pacific Beach. My motivations were undoubtedly confused, but I was clear that this was to be a social event, not a prelude to marriage. We had a good time together, and I knew immediately that this was a person I wanted to see again. From that point things progressed rapidly; and, within a month or two, I found myself proposing to her. Any anxieties about marriage disappeared with the prospect of spending a lifetime with this great person. And I did think of the relationship in terms of a lifetime. One reason I had been so reluctant about contemplating marriage is that I did see it as a long term deal.

Susie reported to me later that my cousin Pose had expressed her enthusiasm for the union, declaring, "We are all so glad. We thought Frank was going to wind up a bachelor." Had I not met Susie, I think I might have. Again, thanks to Ed. He provided the big difference in my life.

Frances Howell and Frank[10] eloped and were married in Laguna Beach on February 14, 1948. Their witnesses were Ed and Dorothy Self, who drove north with them from San Diego. That night the married couple took the overnight Southern Pacific train, the Lark, from Los Angeles to San Francisco. They honeymooned at the Fairmont Hotel on Nob Hill, in San Francisco. The marriage enriched the Sherwood line with a new family, described in the next chapter.

Frank[10] and Frances, the honeymooning couple, at San Francisco's Balalaika restaurant, with its wandering troubadours. This romantic place is long gone.

CHAPTER IV

Frances Howell, Wife of Frank[10] Persons Sherwood, Tenth Generation

Cleo Frances Howell was born in Corsicana, Texas, on November 21, 1926. This is the only time her first name, Cleo, will be used in this book. She detested it and never used it as soon as she became aware there were such things as names for people. In all formal documents she is Frances Howell, without a middle name.

Though her mother insisted she was not responsible, it is a fact that her mother's name was Verna Cleo Robinson. She also disliked the name, never used it, and signed herself as C., to indicate she had a middle name. She swore to her daughter that it was John Virgil, the father, who insisted on it. In any case, two generations of the family were saddled with the name and never used it.

These are the kinds of things that give genealogists nightmares. Having the name right and tracing it is the essential departure point in the pursuit of family history. So it is with some misgiving that we drop the name Cleo; but the real truth is that it should never have been given to Frances in the first place.

A second name problem developed for Frances when she was very young and living with her mother and George Sallee. To this day Frances does not know whether the two were married. In any case Verna was extremely fearful that the child's father might learn where Frances was and take her. There seems no other explanation for Frances having inherited the last name of Sallee, which she carried with increasing impatience through high school. As she prepared for college, she took the independent action of having her name changed back to Howell. As she recalls, her mother had nothing to say about it. In any case, there is no Frances Howell recorded as a member of the class of 1944 at San Diego High School. Frances Sallee is in those files.

Frank[10] complicated things a bit further. Not long after he had begun seeing her, he announced that he did not like the name Frances and wanted to give her another name. Frances was amenable. It was not a matter of great importance to her. At the time she was taking a course in German, and so Frank[10] suggested he call her Susse, German for sweet. Rather quickly that evolved into Susie, and for the last 58 years almost everyone, except her mother, has known Frances as Susie. In essentially all his writings, Frank[10] has referred to his spouse as Susie. At the same time all formal documents, such as property titles, bank statements, and so forth, show her as Frances H. Sherwood.

Hopefully, these words of explanation will enable a future student of Sherwood family history to put the name and person together. Since February 14, 1948, of course, there can be no confusion. She has always been Frances Howell Sherwood.

While more detail will be provided below, the basic facts are that Frances became the first and only daughter of John Virgil Howell and Verna Cleo Robinson, appearing on November 21, 1926. Verna had returned to her Corsicana, Texas, home for the birth, which occurred in the general hospital there.

Frances' parents were young, having married April 7, 1923, when Verna was 18 and John Virgil 23. They lived in Wichita Falls and had been wed about three and one-half years at the time Frances arrived. Verna reported later that she had married primarily to get away from home.

Pictures suggest, however, they were a relatively happy young couple. Instead of solidifying the relationship, Frances' arrival seems to have introduced significant complications. It appears that John Virgil, who worked in the oil fields, was an irresponsible father. In an interview many years later, Verna recalled one time when she arrived with Frances in a small Texas town near where he was working. She was essentially penniless and had no place to stay. Verna fully expected that her husband would provide money and shelter. He never showed up. In a 1988 interview [when Verna was 83], she described the times after Frances' birth in these terms.

Verna and John Virgil on a car in Archer City, Texas, Spring 1926

> After that [Frances' birth], hard times really set in for me. My husband neglected us terribly. He was working in North Texas in the oil fields, and he seemed to forget all about us. He never took care of us in any way. I do not know what I would have done during those years if it had not been for my parents, my father

especially. I stayed with them and had one or two brief periods of employment. But I grew so disgusted that I decided to get a divorce, which I did.[74]

The divorce was final on July 18, 1928, when Frances was less than two. She saw her father only once after that. Though the circumstances were different, Frances and Frank[10] both were reared by their mothers and neither ever really knew a father.

The Robinson Family

Verna Cleo Robinson was the fifth daughter born to Joseph Simpson Robinson and Ollie Victoria Crocker. Verna arrived on March 8, 1905, and followed four sisters: Dovie Lee (b. November 26, 1887), Eddie (b. May 19, 1892), Mae (b. February 14, 1896), and Della (b. October 17, 1898). The first four girls came within 11 years, but it was more than six years later that Verna appeared.

By the time Verna came along, mother Ollie was already in poor health. Never robust, Ollie had apparently felt the burden of carrying and delivering four children. She was not ready to have another. The sad thing is that Ollie told Verna she was not wanted and that Ollie had done all she could to abort the pregnancy. It was something with which Verna lived her entire life and which she never accepted or forgave.

Joseph Simpson Robinson and Ollie Victoria Crocker were married in Cameron, Texas, on May 11, 1886. Verna described the initial meeting of her mother and father:

> My father was working in the fields, plowing, I think. This young woman came walking over the plowed ground to where he was, and introduced herself. They talked. That was the first encounter that my mother and father had. It was somewhere in Milam County, Texas. My mother was an orphan and was living with her aunt. She was young, around 17 or 18. Naturally, she wanted to get out on her own. She knew that my father was working for a man who was a wid-

---

[74] *Grandma Mae's Book.* (Tallahassee, Fl: September, 2000. Prepared by Frank P. Sherwood.) The full transcript of the 1988 interview is included in the book as a separately paged section. The quotation above appears on Page 2. Anyone who wants to know more about Verna Robinson's life will find this book useful because it contains many more family pictures than can be placed in this chapter. It should also be noted that Mae was the name her grandchildren used in referring to her. It occurred because they could not pronounce Verna.

ower, whose wife had died. It was in her mind that she might get the job of being his housekeeper. That is why she came across and spoke to my father. She thought she could get some information.[75]

Subsequently, the two young people were married and had their first child in the following year. The naming of the girls in the Robinson household must have been a fairly major event, as Verna was able to describe in considerable detail the nature of the considerations that accompanied the various names.

Dovie was the oldest. There was a discussion about her name. My father wanted her to be called Dovie. My mother wanted the name of Lee. My father's mother was called Dovie. It was her nickname. Her real name was Julia Ann, but my grandfather called her the pet name of Dovie. So my father wanted his first child named for his mother. Apparently they disagreed on that subject, and some people called her Lee and others called her Dovie. In the family she was always Dovie. She was the oldest. The second girl was called Eddie. I do not know that she ever had another name. I do not think so. The third girl was named Mae. My father wanted her to be called Tiny Mae. He wrote it in the bible, Tiny Mae. But she was never called Tiny. She was always Mae until she got to be rambunctious. Then we called her Bill. I do not know who started with that name. Anyway, she has gone through life as Bill. The fourth girl was Della, who is still living and is now 89 years old. She will be 90 in October. Bill is still living also. She was 92 last February. The fifth child was myself. My mother named me Verna. I do not know where she got the name. It is Greek, as I understand.[76]

Mother Ollie and Father Joseph sitting on porch. No date or place.

Joseph Robinson was descended from families with well-established names in Texas. This was particularly true of his mother, whose father was a Mumford [Montford] and whose mother was a Boren. The Robinsons had originated in South Carolina and had acquired land in Texas. Verna has reported that her

---

[75] Ibid., p. 1
[76] *Loc. Cit.*

This is the family group, with the exception of one sister, Dovie. Father Joseph is holding the youngest daughter, Verna, who is about 2. To his right is Mother Ollie and to his left is daughter Della. Daughter Mae (generally called Bill) is to her mother's right. Daughter Eddie stands behind her mother next to her husband, Ollie Lynch.

grandfather, Thomas Underwood Robinson, had both accumulated and inherited farm land. Unfortunately Joseph Robinson appears not to have been in the line of succession for his father's land. He spent nearly 20 years as a tenant farmer. When he met Ollie, he was a young man working for a neighbor. Making a living as a farmer was very difficult at the time because the crop was cotton, which had plummeted in price. As Verna said, "My father just could not seem to make anything. He was a good farmer, but he finally had to give it up."

Some indication of the difficulties of life in Texas at the time is to be found in Verna's theory of the way she likely contracted tuberculosis (a misfortune that will be treated in greater detail later). When she was quite young, she was sent to live for the summer with her uncle's family [her mother's brother]. There were three children in the family, and the mother was an awful housekeeper. Everything was dirty. All the members of that family later died of tuberculosis. Verna felt that was a place where it was easy for the disease to incubate.

In about 1913 the Robinson family moved to the county seat, Corsicana. They lived for quite some time with the oldest Robinson daughter, Dovie, and her husband. During the period Joseph found only odd jobs. Finally, he obtained janitorial work in a Corsicana milling company, where he stayed for many years. The plant converted cotton into denim. Joseph later said that one of his reasons for moving to Corsicana was to secure better schooling for Verna. The school experience was one of the few things in her early life that Verna found pleasant. She particularly remembered a grammar school teacher, whose name was still in her mind at age 83. In an interview, she observed: "I had one teacher in grammar school whom I remember. She was Greek. Her name was Zuricka Corbey. She got us interested in Greek mythology, and she read Greek mythology to us every Friday afternoon. I will never forget her. She would take us on picnics."[77]

---

[77] Ibid., page 3

By 1927 Ollie had suffered at least two severe strokes, and Verna said she spent about a year after her separation from John Virgil nursing her mother. In 1929 Ollie had a major stroke and two major seizures. She committed suicide on September 15, 1929. Joseph lived to be nearly 100, dying about 11 months short of a century of life, in Fort Worth, Texas. Verna spoke affectionately and positively about her father:

> I would like to say something about my father. He was one of the kindest, most gentle men I have ever known. He was very kind to me and my sisters. Also, he was very kind to his animals on the farm. He had a big argument, almost a fight, with his second son-in-law because he was being cruel to his animals. I have very kindly memories of my father. He was not a great achiever in any sense of the word. He had difficulties making a living at all periods of his life. But he was conscientious, diligent, and caring for his family. I remember all these things very well. I like to think of him in those terms.[78]

It was during the time of her separation from John Virgil and while Verna was spending time at home attending her mother that Verna had her first bout with tuberculosis. She was admitted to the TB hospital in San Angelo in November, 1928, when she was 23. Verna was in the sanitarium for three months and described the experience as "absolutely awful." She checked out long before she was considered well.[79]

[The next events in Verna's life were ones inextricably shared by her daughter. Thus, while this section is focused on Verna, it inevitably intrudes on Frances' life. While certain events that involved both mother and daughter will be described here, some will be revisited later in order more fully to describe Frances' life and experience.]

Verna Goes to California with Frances

After departing the hospital, Verna determined that she and Frances would move on. It was on July 5, 1929 that she and baby Frances departed for California. The circumstances of that trip were such that Verna preferred later they not be recorded; and, if so, not accurately. Her account in the interview was that she went to California to be with her sister Bill and her husband. The prob-

---

[78] *Loc. cit.*

[79] Only in May, 2005, did Frances discover a journal her mother had that contained dates on specific events in her life.

lem with this statement is that her sister Bill was still in Texas. So how, and under what circumstances, did Verna get to California? It is known she was residing in California in September, 1929, because she retained a telegram her sister Bill had sent her in Ventura, announcing their mother's death. The mystery is how a virtually penniless woman with a very small child made it to California.

Enter George Sallee, who lived in Ventura and was apparently on a trip in Texas. It was in his car that Verna and Frances went to California. It's hard to conceive but, given Verna's desperation, Frances thinks Verna may not have known Sallee earlier and was hitchhiking. Everybody hitchhiked in those days; but it would still have been unusual to see a good looking young woman with a small child seeking a ride on the highway. The reality was probably not quite that dramatic, but it is clear that Verna was determined to seek a better life for herself and her child.

Though Verna never mentioned Sallee in her interview, he and Verna apparently lived as man and wife in Ventura. There is a note, whose origin cannot now be ascertained, that they were married on July 5, 1929. The telegram sent by sister Bill reporting the death of their mother was addressed to Mrs. George Sallee in Ventura.

Frances remembers Sallee as not a nice man. He was mean and he beat Verna.

Verna and Susie returned to Texas for a short time after grandmother Ollie's death. The date she recorded for this trip was December 15, 1929, which was the only time Frances remembered seeing her father.

During the time with Sallee, Verna worked in a Ventura cannery. One day she collapsed and was taken to the county hospital. [Her account in the taped interview is a bit different from Frances' memory. Verna said she went to the doctor, who thought she had an ulcer. A test showed it was TB]. In any case, she entered the hospital on November 1, 1932.

With this turn of events, Sallee seems to have disappeared completely from the scene.

Frances was left alone, and there was concern that she also might have contracted tuberculosis. The Catholics took care of her at this point and placed her in the Mother Cabrini institution, labeled a Preventorium, in Glendale, California. Frances was at Mother Cabrini for about six months, by which time Sister Bill had come from Texas with her son Jack.

Verna was in the TB sanitarium for three and one half years, and it was April 8, 1935, when she reunited with her daughter. Verna was very sick and given little prospect of recovery. Only one other person emerged alive from the room she shared at the sanitarium; and that person died a short time later.

Meanwhile, Frances lived with her Aunt Bill and Cousin Jack on welfare in Ventura throughout this period. Though Verna was not yet ready to leave the hospital, Sister Bill had met a man who had invited her to come to Palo Alto, and she was determined to do so. Against medical advice, Verna left the hospital to care for her child. While still on welfare, Frances remembers her mother as unable to work. Verna had no energy and was in bed much of the time.

The couple lived in an apartment in a large house on the Ventura coast. In the same building were three old ladies, who did much to provide support to the little girl. One was Grandma Smith, who smoked a corncob pipe and had come out of the rural North Carolina mountains. She was a marvelous quilter, and Frances spent many hours working with her on quilts. Another old lady loved to walk on the beach and collect seaweed. Frances thinks she was about eight at the time, which would make the year 1935.

As Verna began to regain her health, she apparently got out more. She reports in her taped interview that she met Fred Tyler, who lived in San Diego but was on National Guard duty in the general area of Santa Barbara at the time. It was a relationship of which Susie was quite unaware. The next thing she knew she was put on a train alone and sent to her Aunt Bill in Palo Alto. There she spent the first part of the fifth grade. It is probable the year was 1936.

Meanwhile, Verna had married Fred Tyler January 10, 1937, and had moved to San Diego. Not yet having finished the first semester of the fifth grade, Frances was put on the train again and sent to Los Angeles. There, on April 18, 1937, Verna met her and took her to San Diego, where Frances discovered the reason for the secrecy. It is not known why Verna chose not to tell her daughter of her marriage, but the behavior certainly caused Frances great anguish. To put the best face on it, Verna probably thought that it would simply upset her daughter—which it was bound to do in any case. Frances was settled in an apartment with Verna and Fred, who was then a cook in a local restaurant. Subsequently Fred bought a restaurant on University Ave in San Diego, which also had living quarters. The three resided there until 1941, when they moved into a new house on Law Street in Pacific Beach. This home was an important step in Verna's life. She and Fred now owned a new, modern home.

The restaurant business prospered during World War II, when Fred took over an enterprise in the Mission Hills section of San Diego. The location, whose name was The Orchid and which had been known as a malted milk shop, was a good one. Fred was able to make it into more of a restaurant. Difficulties arose in the marriage, however; and one result was the sale of The Orchid. During the war Verna worked for a year as a ration clerk in the Enforcement section of the U.S. Office of Price Administration (OPA), where she encountered Mercedes Verdugo, who ran a children's shop in the Hillcrest area. They became good friends; and Verdugo persuaded Verna to open a similar kind of store in Pacific

Beach, which must have occurred in 1945. Verna owned the building, located at 4460 Cass Street, in which she located the Cradle Shop.

Meanwhile, she and Fred were back together; and he was working as a chef at local restaurants. In the academic year, 1944-45, Frances was enrolled at the University of California, Berkeley.

Later, Fred repurchased the restaurant on University Ave. He was involved in a grueling, six day week undertaking. He sometimes stayed in the apartment behind the restaurant and at other times made the long commute back to Pacific Beach.

In 1950 Verna and Fred decided to sell the house in Pacific Beach. They moved to an older, larger, and more comfortable home in La Mesa, a small town east of San Diego. That seemed to be a happy time for them. It was a fairly placid life, and they appeared to have found considerable enjoyment in each other.

Then came the huge blow. At age about 50 Fred suffered a massive heart attack. The year was 1951; and again Verna's life [she was then 46] was torn apart. Frances and Frank[10] had moved to Los Angeles in 1949, and so Verna had no real family in San Diego. She settled in an apartment on Cass street in Pacific Beach and proceeded to lead a quiet life there. She closed the Cradle Shop in 1954.

In the period 1954-64 Verna held three jobs. The first was with Iller's department store in La Jolla, where she worked in the children's department; and the second was with a large construction company, where she was the accountant. When that company was sold and the headquarters moved, she secured a job in La Jolla with an interesting young man, whose name was Cornish. He was a member of an extremely wealthy family; and it was his job to manage its very substantial assets. A thoroughly nice man, he became interested in Verna's financial situation and got her to thinking about investing. As she reports in her taped interview, he took her to Merrill Lynch to open an account and then told her where to place her money. He guided her into mutual funds, which were only then beginning to emerge as investment vehicles. With her fine mind, it was no surprise that Verna developed a strong interest in stocks and followed them avidly the rest of her life. There is little doubt that Comish's influence was tremendously important in enabling Verna to expand her modest assets to a sufficient scale that they provided her a comfortable living.

Not long after Ed Self's mother (Dickie), died, his father (Harry) began to see Verna. The courtship was brief. Verna and Harry were married in Laguna Beach in 1964, not much more than a year after Dickie's death. Verna moved to the Self home at 2820 Kalmia Place. It seemed like a neat arrangement for two people who had lost their mates and who shared a lot of associations.

But the marriage did not work out. There were no hard feelings, and in her taped interview Verna said she and Harry were simply incompatible. In 1967 she moved out of the Kalmia house and took up residence in an apartment on Park Blvd., just north of Balboa Park. She lived there for 13 years. Verna and Harry were never divorced. They continued to see and enjoy each other. They went out to dinner, played golf, and so forth. His death was another loss for her. As she reports in her interview, she was the last person to see Harry alive. Harry left one important gift to her, the widow's share of his Social Security. It provided an important financial base for her.

She continued to live on Park Blvd but found it increasingly difficult to cope with many of life's demands. Frances had urged her for years to move back east where she would have some support. Finally, in 1980, Verna consented; and she was established in a duplex in Charlottesville, Va., where Frances and Frank[10] were living. It should be noted that Verna accompanied Frances and Frank[10] when they drove east in the summer, 1968. So she knew something about Charlottesville. At that time she was 63, and she already seemed old and frail.

When Frank[10] was offered a position on the faculty of Florida State University in Tallahassee, Florida, in 1982, Verna was consulted before a decision about moving was made. She was agreeable, and so the family went south in August, 1982. At the time Verna was 77. For the next 15 years she resided in the Meridian apartments in Tallahassee, had her own car, and led a peaceful, quiet life. By 1996 it was becoming apparent that a completely independent life was no longer feasible; and, in the following year, she moved to Westminster Oaks, a senior retirement community in Tallahassee. She was 92. She fared rather well there, developed warm associations with a number of other residents, and did quite satisfactorily health-wise. It should be noted, however, that Verna was never really happy. There was always something in life that was unsatisfactory.

One of the last pictures of Verna, taken in early 2000, with great granddaughter Lindsay on left and great granddaughter Emily on right.

In the Spring 2000, she fell during the night in her apartment. She broke her hip and suffered severe trauma because she was unattended for several hours. Now 95, Verna handled the hip replacement well and seemed clearly on the way to recovery. In the hospital, however, she contracted a virus [colloquially known as C-dif] that proved lethal. It deprived her of her appetite, rendered her listless, and she ultimately died on August 8, 2000, in the clinic at Westminster Oaks. In her lifetime she had experienced many physical problems, not just tuberculosis, and she managed her way through all of them. Her self-discipline was undoubtedly an important factor in enabling her to live a long life that was quite comfortable over the last 50 years.

John Virgil and the Howell Family

When John Virgil and Verna separated, he moved immediately to Corpus Christie, Texas. His obituary reports that he had lived there since 1927. In all likelihood Frances was less than a year old when her father left. His activities after that time most emphatically did not involve his daughter.

John Virgil was the fourth of 10 children born to Lemuel Carroll Howell and Mary Lee Anderson on February 1, 1900 in Lindale, Texas.

Both parents were relatively recent arrivals in Texas from Arkansas. Lemuel was born in Amity, Arkansas, on August 31, 1872, and Mary Lee was probably born there also, though the record shows her birth only in Arkansas. Her date of birth was November 6, 1875. The mothers of both John Virgil's parents were also Arkansas-born, but Lemuel's father was from Mississippi. Nothing is known of the origins of Mary Lee's father, F.M. Anderson.

Lemuel and Mary Lee were married in Amity, Arkansas, on February, 1890, ten years before John Virgil was born; and so it is probable the couple had lived in Texas only in the decade of the 1890s. Lemuel is said to have died of apoplexy, generally regarded as a stroke, on September 21, 1925, in Corsicana, where he was pastor of the Corsicana Baptist church. He was only 53. Mary Lee lived another 23 years, dying in Corsicana, Texas, in December, 1948 at the age of 73. Frances had contact with her Howell grandmother once. She had come to San Diego after World War II to visit a son who was in the Navy.

John Virgil's obituary reports that he spent his work career with the Atlantic Richfield company and retired in 1963 as a pumper-gauger. He was then 63.

In Corpus Christie he raised a second family. He and his wife Georgia had a daughter, Mary Katherine, and he apparently adopted his wife's son. In 1998 the adopted son, Dale Howell, was listed in the Corpus Christie telephone book. No address was provided for the daughter, identified in the obituary as Mrs. Billy Fox.

John Virgil died on June 27, 1973, with the immediate cause myocardial infarction brought on by severe pulmonary emphysema, according to his death certificate. It seems clear that he was a lifelong smoker. At the time of his death, John Virgil was living in Robstown, Texas, a suburb of Corpus Christie. He had six grandchildren and four great grandchildren.

Frances' First Ten Years

The following section has been the most difficult to write in this entire history. That is because it deals with a very unhappy childhood. If Frances were asked what she would prefer, it would be that this part of her life be overlooked.

Her feeling is not surprising. It is much more uplifting to recall the good parts of a life rather than the bad. We have talked with a number of friends about this. Few said they would tell even their children about parts of their lives they would rather forget, much less commit such experiences to print, where they would be available to all. Yet histories like this are about real people, whose lives always have some blemishes. Further, as will be seen in what follows, Frances' life is far from sad. It is a success story.

Why did things go so terribly wrong in her first decade? The big problem was that her father, Virgil, was not ready to assume the responsibilities of marriage and parenthood. That led to a divorce when Frances was less than two years old. Further, as though the disengagement from her father were not a large enough source of stress, the trip to California and residence there with a penniless mother and an unpleasant man must have been unsettling, certainly for a very small child.

It does not seem that Frances suffered any real physical privations. One way or another, she seems to have had adequate food and shelter.

The stresses were psychological and emotional. At some point in her early childhood, she recognized that she did not have a father. He had abandoned her. A child's recognition of that reality is exceedingly painful. We all want to believe that our parents truly love us and care for us. The rejection hit Frances particularly hard. She never forgave her father for having deserted her so completely and for having had so little interest in her well-being. Years later he wrote her a letter apologizing for his behavior. From her perspective, forgiveness was impossible, but she did respond, saying she forgave him.

As a small child, Frances was entirely dependent on her mother. But Verna was not a strong resource. Before she went to California, she had contracted tuberculosis and had left a Texas hospital before she was cured. That illness deposited her in a Ventura hospital for three and a half years, a hospital from which almost no one left alive. Even before she was stricken, though, Verna was working very hard at menial jobs.

It was when Verna was admitted to the TB hospital that things took a decided turn for the worst. About four years of age, Frances was left with no one. The small child had no place to go. Rather remarkably, the Catholic church [probably because of the intercession of welfare workers] came to the rescue. Remarkable because Verna was not a Catholic or involved in any organized religion. The Catholics enrolled

Frances in the Mother Cabrini institution, as reported earlier, largely because it was feared the small child might have contracted TB from her mother.

Frances spent six months at Mother Cabrini, where her physical needs were reasonably well met. But it was a forbidding place, made more so by the profound dedication to Catholic doctrine and practices. What Frances recalls as the epitome of religious excess was the insistence that she take a bath in a nightgown. She experienced isolation for two weeks after her arrival. But perhaps the most traumatic aspect of the Mother Cabrini experience was simply not knowing what would happen next. Would she ever see her mother again? If not, what was to happen to her? Was she destined to spend many years at dreary Mother Cabrini?

Frances at age 3 in Ventura, California

At this point Frances' fortunes took a turn for the better. The Robinson family back in Corsicana recognized that something had to be done. Verna's child could not be left alone and vulnerable. Verna's sister, Bill, who was always unpredictable and willing to take chances, came to California with her son Jack. They immediately went on welfare in Ventura and brought Frances back into the family fold. A small element of security returned to Frances' life.

Among other things, Frances found in her Aunt Bill someone who clearly loved her and was nurturing. She was far more demonstrative in her affections than was Verna, who was reserved and unwilling to express emotion, even to her daughter.

This interlude turned out to be relatively brief, however. Bill had met a man who invited her and son Jack to come live with him in Palo Alto. There was more turbulence for Frances. In the end, Verna left the hospital early and assumed the care of her little daughter. The two were on welfare and the small child now had a sick mother on her hands. It was at this time that three old ladies living in the same apartment building were important sources of nurture and support for Frances, who was about eight. The year was 1935.

But this was not the end of upheaval for Frances. As was reported earlier, Verna had married again and had summoned Frances, who traveled from Palo Alto to Los Angeles. There she met her mother, and the two proceeded to San Diego. The whole experience was unsettling. Just as she was about to enter the fifth grade in Ventura in the fall 1936, Frances was put on the train for Palo Alto. Then, a few months later and after being with her Aunt Bill for a semester, she was back on the train again, heading south. In this period Frances had no idea what was going on and more particularly what was happening to her mother. Physically, life was pleasant enough but there was anxiety. Where was her mother? What was going on?

In Los Angeles Frances had another big shock. Verna told her she had married again, and they were on their way to San Diego, where they would reside with a man Frances had never met. It was hard for a very smart eight-year-old to understand why she had been kept so much in the dark. Yet it characterized her relationship with Verna, who was typically inclined to keep things to herself. Verna worried greatly about Frances' physical needs but there was almost no interest in her emotional requirements. For Frances this was particularly difficult because the years of turbulence had left her highly self-reliant. What she most needed was information on which she could act rationally. And that was what her mother denied her.

With the trip to San Diego, the first chapter in Frances' life came to an end. And just as well. It had not been happy. She had progressed well in school, but her frequent moves limited her ability to make fast friends. Further, she was a rather sickly child, afflicted with glandular problems. To make things even worse, her legs had been run over by an errant Model T Ford, with more time spent on the sick list.

The only school experience she remembers with fondness involved the Catholic school at the Ventura Mission, which she chose to attend after the six months in Mother Cabrini. She had become attached to the Catholic church, though not enamored of it, and thus preferred the Catholic to a public school. She remembers herself as about the only non-Catholic in the school. "When it came time for Confession, I was the only kid left in the classroom," she recalled. Unlike many of her classmates, the eight-year-old made the long walk on Sunday to attend Mass.

Her best friends were the Nuns who were her teachers, not the other students. "I knew my Catechism. The Nuns liked me."

San Diego: A New Life with Fred Tyler

Mother Verna had made an exceptionally good choice in her new husband, Fred Tyler. He made it possible for both mother and daughter to embark on a life of much greater economic and emotional stability. Welfare was a thing of the past. Before moving on, however, it is important to understand that welfare at that time was a far more significant part of the average American's life than it is today. Many of the support programs that exist in 2006 were not there; and at times average Americans found themselves desperately needing help. California was in many respects the best state in which to receive such supports. Not only were the benefits better but welfare administration was much more professionalized. Further, the welfare workers had the support of Californians, most of whom saw themselves barely removed from welfare. They generally felt that welfare recipients were people who had encountered a little bad luck and providing welfare was what good neighbors did. While there was a stigma to welfare even then, it had nothing like the bite that came later. It was a time when a good government, like that of California, took care of its people, especially those temporarily in trouble. Verna was a good example of the way in which proud people returned to the role of contributing citizens. For the last 65 years of her life, she was a taxpaying, responsible member of the society, never coming close to needing welfare.

Fred Tyler, who can best be described as unassuming, would be surprised to read the statement in this book that he really changed the lives of two people, Verna and Frances. That, however, is what the facts argue.

He may have had even a harder younger life than either Verna or Frances. The general belief is that he was born illegitimate in London and that his mother [with whom he always maintained contact] had to send him to Canada as a young boy to work on a farm. He labored very hard, got little education, and had one major physical mishap. He broke both legs chasing a pig. When he had enough, he escaped over the border into Ohio and there enlisted in the Marines. From that time on, he was born in Ohio.

Fred and Frances on outing in Balboa Park, San Diego

His Marine service involved a period in China; and it also seemed to provide him occupational credentials as a cook. When his enlistment was up, Fred found himself in San Diego and decided to stay there. He got a job as a cook, enlisted in the National Guard, and was on a bivouac in Santa Barbara when he met Verna.

The year of their marriage, 1937, has to be regarded as close to the bottom of the Depression. It is therefore no small miracle that he had regular employment and had the means to provide his new family an apartment, at Park Boulevard and University Avenue. The building was not luxurious, but it was solidly middle class. Most San Diegans would have been happy to have such lodging. One has to conclude that Fred was very good at his craft, very hard working, and a quality team player. Frances remembers that he was a particularly talented pastry cook. He had to have a lot of positive assets because this was a time when people were bidding down the wages for a job, offering to work for less than the going rate.

Not only did Fred bring an economic stability to the lives of Verna and Frances, but he was a calming influence. Frances says she always regarded him as friend, not a father. "My mother had to control my life, and there was no place for Fred in that relationship," she recalled. "But there were certainly times when he helped me work around my mother." Frances' laudatory assessment of Fred focused on three characteristics: generous, supportive, and all around good. Further, she remembered, "He was on my side."

The Restaurant on University Avenue

The economic status of the little family was advanced in less than a year when Fred and Verna purchased a small restaurant on University avenue, just a few blocks away from their apartment. With 18 stools arrayed around a counter, it may be a little much to describe it as a restaurant. Despite its physical limitations, however, the hard-working Fred Tyler offered three meals a day, six days a week. He was there from dawn until eight or later at night.

The staff for this very substantial operation was small, with only one waitress and a dishwasher to aid him. Verna, still low on energy and recovering from her TB, functioned essentially as the business manager. She effectively handled all the tasks required of a small enterprise, even in those simpler days. Further, they saved money by moving into an older house situated behind the restaurant. Those were not days when any small business was doing really well, but they made ends meet.

Though she was now moving among children who had more than she, life had become far more stable for Frances. She had a dog and a friend in Fred, who was very happy to do things with her, though the outings were limited by his heavy work schedule. Perhaps her biggest complaint was that the Florence school, in which she was enrolled for the second half of the fifth grade, was a very long walk, both from the apartment and then from the restaurant.

Roosevelt Junior High School

With the completion of her elementary school education at Florence in 1938, school became a much more attractive proposition. She now attended Roosevelt Junior High, which was a much shorter walk and where she also began to make neighborhood friends. She found Roosevelt, as had her future husband Frank[10] six years earlier, a challenging and stimulating learning environment. It was a place where she felt she could put down some roots. There were two aspects of the Roosevelt experience that she recalls decades later.

She was painfully shy, and it was virtually impossible for her to say hello to anyone, even in the halls. Facing her difficulty, she exhibited the behavior that was very characteristic of her later life. She bit the bullet and determinedly approached students she hardly knew, just to say hello.

She remembers an occasion in a history class with Miss Henrietta Rose when it came her turn to appear before the class and make a presentation. She couldn't have been in a better situation because Miss Rose, old and diminutive, was beloved by everyone in the school for her supportiveness. Frances recalls that she trembled visibly as she stood before the class, by Miss Rose's desk. Then she felt Miss Rose's hand taking her hand and gripping it. That was real reassurance. She got through the rest of the presentation without difficulty.

Another long-time characteristic was revealed on another occasion at Roosevelt. Even at age 12, she revealed her streak of independence. The proper thing for all the girls in her class to do was to take home economics. But Frances had no interest in the subject. After considerable wrangling, she got herself freed from Home Economics and took Print Shop, which she loved.

The High School Years, 1941-1944, within a Context of War

Frances was young when she completed Roosevelt and entered on a new educational adventure, matriculation at the venerable and formidable San Diego High School in downtown San Diego. With 3000 students, it was by far the largest and best resourced of the institutions in the San Diego school system. Frances was still 14 when she entered the ivied halls of the school, fondly known as the Gray Castle. And that meant she would graduate when she was still 16.

When Frances was living behind the restaurant, transportation to San Diego High was easy. Street cars on University Avenue and Park Boulevard provided a quick ride. But those good days came to an end in 1942 [during Frances' first year in high school]. In that year Verna and Fred built a very nice home excessively distant from the high school, in Pacific Beach. Frances now resided in the area served by La Jolla High School. However, she would have nothing to do with changing schools. As far as anyone knew, she continued to live at the location of the restaurant. The major problem, of course, was transportation. She now had a one-hour bus ride each day on vehicles crowded with wartime workers.

Not only was the bus ride onerous, but Frances lived in constant fear she would be found out. A substitute teacher at San Diego High boarded the bus frequently, and Frances enlisted the cooperation of her regular bus compatriots to see that she was well hidden from the teacher. That ride, with its attendant fears of discovery, constituted the worst part of the SDHS experience.

In high school Frances developed a close friendship with Norma Benbrook that carried over to the first year of college. What particularly tied them together was music. Norma was an accomplished musician, and Frances was a willing learner. They attended many concerts and managed to spend considerable time at Thearle's music store on Broadway, where they could listen to records.

When she was a junior, Frances had her first real boy friend, a senior. They were a "steady" couple for much of the year. What was special about this relationship was that he could commandeer sufficient gasoline to come to Pacific Beach to take her out. The time was 1942-43, when the United States was fully engaged in war. There was virtually no gasoline available. But this was a case where the boy's father was engaged in a war-related enterprise and had a few extra coupons. After his graduation, her boy friend went into a wartime Naval program, the V-12, and was posted at Rice University. When he came home at Christmas, 1943, Frances discovered the two had drifted apart and broke off the relationship.

Frances' Graduation Picture 1944

That Christmas was a busy time. Virtually all able-bodied men and women were either in the military or involved in war production. Yet the Christmas mail had to be processed. Who was to do it? High school people, teachers and students, stepped into the void. Frances recalls two hectic weeks at the post office, working side by side with her teachers. It was a good example of the way in which everyone got together during World War II to get the job done.

There is a picture in Frances' album that records one of her pleasant experiences in high school. It captures several members of the Biological Sciences Club arrayed around a car on a primitive road in scrub woods. The Club enrolled students who had a fascination for wild life and enjoyed the search for them. Much time was spent trudging on the mud flats at low tide in Mission Bay. One of the members of this intrepid group achieved some national notoriety. Roy Walford was a whiz in mathematics. With a partner, and as a very young man, he "broke the bank" at Las Vegas. He went on to become a doctor; was the resident physician at the

Frances [at left] with fellow students on a Science Biology Club outing.

Biosphere, an experiment in living in a closed environment; and later concentrated on issues of aging. Unfortunately, his research did him little good. He died when he was in his seventies.

Frances remembers San Diego High School as providing a highly stimulating and challenging learning environment. She says she gained from essentially all her teachers. Three for whom she had particularly fond memories are Virginia Gilloon, who taught Social Studies; Meave Sharman, whose responsibility was Latin, and Ruth P. Weiss, head of the English Department, who selected her to write the graduation ceremony in verse.

At a brief stop in Carlsbad when Frances was eloping with Frank[10], the couple encountered Mary Phillippi, the long-time Senior A adviser at San Diego High. Miss Phillippi, who had herself acquired a husband, was particularly delighted to see Frances, a member of the Senior A committee she had advised three years earlier. The reason for her enthusiasm was she had completely lost track of Frances Sallee; and so it was a thrill to see her emerge as a bright and happy Frances Howell, on her way to marital bliss.

Frances was obviously in the college preparatory track at San Diego High [which probably enrolled less than half the total student body]; and, while she has no idea of her grade point average, she assumes that it was either B or B+. It had to be at about that level because she had no trouble later with admission to the state's most prestigious university, the University of California at Berkeley.

Frances graduated at a massive ceremony in Balboa Stadium, adjacent to the high school, in June, 1944.

On to College in the Fall, 1944

There was no doubt that Frances would attend college; but she realized that the family exchequer, while having improved significantly, still very much limited her options. She felt the best she could manage was the University of California at Los Angeles [from which she ultimately received her degree in June, 1950]. Her plan was to live with her Aunt Bill and make the long commute from El Monte to Westwood. Her experience at San Diego High had made her more accepting of extended travel times.

Her friend, Norma, had other ideas. She was going to Berkeley and was anxious that Frances join her there. Frances was dubious and felt her mother would never agree. To her great surprise, Norma was able to convince Verna that Berkeley was the place for her daughter.

So a great adventure began in October, 1944, just as the United States was beginning to savor triumph in World War II. Berkeley and San Francisco were, however, very much on a wartime footing. Frances and Norma secured lodging in a fraternity house that had been turned over to the girls for the duration. It was a liberating experience for Frances. Though not yet 17, she was ready to set her own course and to be free from a controlling mother. Not only did she have good times with her roommates, but there were plenty of young military people who found the university a great place to see girls and at least think about fun. Further, she was able to go with one friend to her parents' farm, where food ration stamps were not relevant. There was plenty of milk, eggs, and butter, those elements of good food that were disgustingly lacking from wartime diets.

Frances found Berkeley a demanding place, but she did well enough to survive. Her biggest problem was in Psychology, a discipline in which she had a great interest and was a possible major. The class followed a customary Berkeley pattern, a very large lecture class with a professor and then small group sessions with a teaching assistant. The orientation of the class toward science, with much emphasis on research findings, also made the subject matter difficult for a young freshman. Worst of all, the teaching assistant was a total bust as a teacher. Frances never felt she understood what was going on and was relieved that she did not fail the course.

Well aware that her mother would be monitoring her expenditures carefully, Frances not only kept her spending to a minimum but got herself a job. Attendance at the University itself cost almost nothing. There was no tuition and fees were very low. There were few universities, and none of its quality, as easy to finance as Berkeley. Essentially, any additional costs were a result of living away from home.

Frances got a job with a special kind of enterprise at the university, the Institute of Public Administration. Its founder and still its leader in 1944-45 was Sam May, a warm and highly regarded figure in California government. He had made the Institute a place to which the governments of the state could turn for help in developing and implementing policies. Frances was a receptionist and had a chance to be a part of a really remarkable outreach program at Berkeley.

Frances [at left] with fellow students on a Science Biology Club outing.

When Frances went home for Christmas, 1994, she encountered a sad and disturbing development. Verna and Fred had separated. Not having been present when things disintegrated, she had little feel for what had happened—except that there was another woman.

By the time she returned in June, 1945, Fred and Verna were back together, but Verna then made a stunning and startling pronouncement. Frances would not be returning to Berkeley. She had spent too much money there. As Frances saw the situation then, as well as many years later, there was no arguing with Verna. She had made up her mind, and there was no negotiation.

This was a tremendous blow for Frances. She had loved Berkeley, both as a social and as an academic venue. She felt she had matured a great deal, largely because she had more freedom to do things in her own way. And she valued Berkeley for its academic quality. It meant a lot to have a degree from such a fine institution.

It is unclear what Verna was thinking. Frances does not recall that her mother took an interest in her Berkeley experience or even asked her how she felt about it. She acted without considering her daughter's feelings. Was there a strong imperative for such an action? Frances does not know. There was nothing said about the family financial situation, and there seems to be no evidence it had deteriorated. It may have been that Verna saw no real difference between Berkeley and San Diego State College, where Frances could live at home and save lodging and transportation costs. Frances later felt that the breakup with Fred may have had some repercussions. Verna simply wanted to have her daughter close by. In any case, the inability to return to Berkeley was certainly one of the major disappointments in Frances' young life.

Dutifully, Frances undertook studies at San Diego State College in the Fall, 1945. It was done without enthusiasm. Much of her optimism and zest for the future was lost. In many respects she was marking time, attending classes and helping her mother in the children's store Verna had opened in Pacific Beach. Fred, meanwhile, had taken a job as a chef at the U.S. Grant Hotel in downtown San Diego.

This was the circumstance when Ed Self began to sell *North Shores Sentinel* advertisements to Verna in the fall, 1946. His contact with Frances was only occasional; but, as was reported in the last chapter, he was impressed with her. He saw her as a future wife for his partner, Frank[10]. He hired her for a part-time job at the paper partly because he thought she would be good and also because he wanted to bring the two together. The story of the courtship has been reported in the previous chapter, and all that needs to be reaffirmed here is that Frances Howell and Frank[10] Sherwood were married in Laguna Beach, California, on February 14, 1948.

CHAPTER V

Frank[10] Persons Sherwood and Frances Howell: The Linkage of Two Families and the Birth of Two Children

In the previous two chapters the lives of the two people at the heart of the 10th generation Sherwood family were detailed. The intent of this chapter is to reveal the nature of the family activity of the Sherwoods roughly from the period 1948, when Frank[10] and Frances were married, until their two children Jeff[11] and Robin[11] were well established in college and generally on their own, roughly 1973-74. The first child did not appear, however, until 1953; and so the real family period, when there were parents and children, had a duration of about 20 years.

The five years before the appearance of children provided the base for future events. Hence it is important to provide detail on that period. The professional experience of Frank[10] also requires brief treatment, largely to provide a context for the activities of this family of four.

The major objective of this chapter is, though, to provide a sense of how the family lived in the period 1953 to 1973. Fortunately, we have a resource that carries us beyond bare factual recall. Volumes

Frank[10] checks out a new house they bought but never occupied with the two kids and Mother Mildred about 1955.

were prepared when both Jeff[11] and Robin[11] turned 40. The idea was to provide as complete a picture of their lives up to that point as possible. Jeff[11] wrote on his sister and Robin[11] reported on her brother. In addition Mother Frances and Father Frank[10], as well as many others, contributed their recollections. The books are true collectors' items. Since our purpose was to provide a sense of dynamic family activity, excerpts were taken from Mother Frances on both children, son Jeff[11] on Robin[11] and Robin[11] on her brother. It was felt that these three observers had the most intimate view of what really went on in the household.

This chapter concludes with a report on the patriarchs, Frank[10] and Frances, since they became "empty nesters" in the mid-70s.

-101-

Momentous Events: The Sale of the North Shores Sentinel

As soon as Frank[10] and Frances returned from their honeymoon, she became a major part of *North Shores Sentinel* operations. She did about everything except the printing. Frank[10] found, too, that she was an excellent manager. She picked up many administrative matters that Ed and he had let slide. One problem, however, was that she had lost some of the easy rapport she had with the print shop staff, particularly the linotype operator, a very strong union man. He told her things would never be the same. She had "sold out" to management.

Even before the honeymoon, Partners Ed Self and Frank[10] had begun to discuss their future intensively. They were having real cash flow problems at the newspaper but not because revenues were declining. It was quite the opposite. They were selling more advertising than ever, which meant increasing amounts of money were owed them. They simply did not have the resources to extend growing amounts of credit. While they saw tough days ahead, both partners believed they could ride out these problems, somehow or other.

Finances, therefore, did not constitute the real issue. What they found really difficult to handle were their feelings about the newspaper and the community. For Frank[10] much of the idealism of owning and operating a newspaper had vanished. He and Ed had attended a meeting of the California Newspaper Publishers Association in Los Angeles and learned that its board was recommending that the Association take a stand on 5,000 of the 7,000 bills being proposed in the next State legislative session. How could that be? They asked themselves. Certainly there cannot be that many matters coming before the State legislature with real public consequence. What they learned was that the publishers saw themselves as running a business, not an enterprise with public interest goals. They were against anything that cost them money or imposed restrictions on their ability to optimize their interests.

While they thought they had done well with the *Sentinel*, Frank[10] and Ed became aware that it would take years to build sufficient capital to purchase a really major newspaper. The question was whether they were prepared to devote a significant portion of their lives to enterprises and communities that were not likely to afford them any real satisfaction. Ed was disappointed, too, that the *Sentinel* offered him virtually no opportunity to express his creativity and particularly to pursue his interests in graphic design. Frank[10] 's concerns were more mundane. He simply did not like the conflict that was a part of running a newspaper in a small community. There was often anger directed toward matters of little consequence, and it stole time from things that were important. He came to realize that he was quite a private person. There was a reason he had insisted on eloping. Finally, he began to wonder whether he would find satisfaction in operating even a major newspaper. Many of the same kinds of forces would be operating; and so he wondered if he were heading in the right direction.

As a result of these ruminations, Ed and Frank[10] concluded that they should move into downtown San Diego and undertake to launch an organization that would engage in a variety of publishing ventures. At the time they did not have a clear idea what they might be, though they were aware that *San Diego* magazine, which had been published by the San Diego Chamber of Commerce before the war, had not been revived.

Having made a general decision about their future, the next step was to seek the sale of the *Sentinel*. Ed had had previous contact with Vince Manno, a member of a large newspaper brokerage firm in New York. Manno was willing to take on the task of finding a buyer, and a price of $50,000 was set for the newspaper. That amount was two and one-half times what the partners had paid 18 months earlier. Quickly, Manno identified a buyer, whose last name was Cormack and who quickly arranged to inspect the property. Cormack seemed to have access to considerable wealth and appeared to have even less understanding of small town newspapers than Frank[10] and Ed had. He seemed to be even more casual in his inspection of the property than they had been.

Frank[10] writes about the negotiation:

> Furthermore, he [Cormack] was strange. Ed handled much of the contact and told me about a time at the bar in the La Valencia hotel in La Jolla. Cormack was anxious to have a drink, and Ed accompanied him. The prospective owner summoned the bartender and instructed him, "Two double martinis." Ed said he found the behavior arrogant and insensitive because he thought Cormack was ordering for him. He was quickly disabused, however, when Cormack asked, "And what will you have?" It was apparent that Cormack had a problem beyond his ignorance of small newspapers. He appeared to be an alcoholic.
>
> But he was sober enough to know that he wanted the paper and to drive us down a bit on the price. We agreed to a figure of $40,000, half in cash and the other half to be paid with interest in monthly installments over five years.
>
> The deal went through; and it was April, 1948, when Cormack took control of the *Sentinel*. We had nothing about which to be embarrassed. Our strategy had worked perfectly. In a little more than 18 months we had doubled our money. We felt very good about ourselves.
>
> That was before we talked to a Dartmouth friend, who was an accountant in San Pedro. It turned out that we had committed a colossal blunder, the first of two that would happen in about a year. We had run afoul of the Federal tax col-

lector. Income taxes were steeply progressive in those days, climbing to 80%. Even in the best of circumstances, a substantial share of our profit would have been taken by Uncle Sam. But there was another wrinkle in the tax code. If the down payment were more than a third, the tax on all the profit became due immediately. Since we had obtained a 50% down payment, we had a huge tax bill. We ended up having far less for our new venture than was true when we took over the *Sentinel*. Also, there was the obligation to my mother. She was quite willing, though, to recoup her investment through Cormack's monthly payments. As it turned out, he was careful to discharge his obligation; and I think he paid off the debt well before it was due.[80]

Their straitened financial situation meant that Ed and Frank[10] had to rethink their next steps. Now that the two were free of their business obligations, Frank[10] and Ed found their interests were beginning to diverge. Ed had become interested only in publishing and wanted nothing to do with machinery. Frank[10] felt that he had to have a printing operation to satisfy his ambitions. Ed settled on the idea of starting a new *San Diego* magazine, a title, incidentally, still held by the Chamber of Commerce. It was agreed that the two would jointly own the magazine but that Ed would devote his full energies to it and thereby receive a salary from it.

Robin[11] is adorned with leis as she and Judy greet Frank[10] on his 1956 return from Hawaii. Note the mumu.

Momentous Events: The New Enterprises and a Disastrous Fire

Frank[10] set out to find himself a printing operation and did discover one that seemed adequate for the purpose. It was located in the outbuildings of an old house in San Diego, which was not a suitable venue. A vacant furniture warehouse was leased in uptown San Diego. It was a fairly massive building with plenty of space on the ground floor for the printing operation. Various other activities were housed in a catacomb of cubicles essentially suspended from the

---

[80] Frank P. Sherwood, *Autobiography,* in draft.

sides of the building. The site was not impressive, but it suited the production needs of the new enterprise quite well.

There were aspects of the printing operation that involved various people and were somewhat complicated, and a detailing of them will not serve any real purpose here. The point is that Frances and Frank[10] managed the printing operation, with some bookkeeping help from Frank's uncle who had retired as a doctor and was pleased to get involved. The enterprise started well enough in the late summer, 1948, and it looked like a going business had been launched.

Meanwhile, Ed was working diligently on the first issue of *Magazine San Diego* [He switched the words so as to avert any legal attack by the Chamber of Commerce], which was composed in the Sherwood shop, the Benj. Franklin Press, with the press work to be handled elsewhere in the city. The first issue appeared in October, 1948. Frank[10] describes it in the following terms: "It was truly a thing of beauty. It was not a second rate, small town publication. It rivaled national journals like *Vogue, Holiday,* and *New Yorker.* Ed had wrought a small miracle, and it was because of the many, many hours he spent in the print shop to get displays just the way he wanted them. [Again, it is critical to know that he was working with lead type and zinc engravings, not with the computer software and offset printing that is available today.] As I examined what Ed had done, I realized that he and I were very different. I could never match his imaginative handling of graphics. As it turned out, that magazine became his life's work."[81]

Frances and Frank[10] were working long hours, but their problems were eased by the fact that they resided only a few blocks away from the plant. Mildred had sold the house in Pacific Beach and bought a two-unit property just half a block from her old flower shop. She occupied one of the houses and Frank[10] and Frances took over the other. As might be expected, Mildred did a lot of the cooking and helped out in other ways. Meanwhile, she had gone back into the real estate business.

By the end of 1948 San Diego was in the grip of a very serious recession. And the new enterprise was encountering a familiar problem, inadequate operating capital. Yet these difficulties seemed momentary. Business was still fairly good, and the future looked promising. With respect to the magazine, there was no expectation that it would be immediately profitable. The magazine had attracted a lot of approval, however, and its advertising prospects were very good.

It was about that time that Frank[10] has observed that he made a second "dumb decision" in less than a year. He describes it and subsequent events:

---

[81] *Loc. cit.*

It came in a meeting with our insurance agent, who argued that we needed coverage in two critical areas: (a) property liability and (b) business interruption. The session came at a time when I was feeling particularly pressed financially. I didn't have much issue with the idea of business interruption insurance; but I thought we needed to take a risk until our finances were in better shape. I really rejected the idea of property liability insurance, apparently reasoning entirely from my modest experience with car insurance. I remember asking the agent, "How in the world can we harm someone else's property? Do you think there is a possibility we might drive this building into someone's auto?" I don't remember his even attempting to answer my stupid question. A smarter agent might have saved me our later problems.

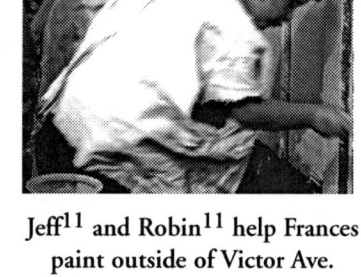

Jeff[11] and Robin[11] help Frances paint outside of Victor Ave. House. 1957

In any case we did not expand our insurance coverage beyond our own physical equipment. Things had not changed much by April, 1949, except that Susie and I may have been working harder. It was a night and day proposition. Several weeks earlier, we had to lay off a young man who operated our large newspaper press. Then, as the work mounted, we called him back to begin work very early in the morning, about 5 a.m. He was feeding sheets into the large flat bed press, where the paper passed on a conveyor, finally moving under a gas flame before dropping into a hopper. The phone rang, and he responded as he had in the past. He got down from the press and went to the office to answer it. He did not know that we had a telephone mounted on the press and that he did not have to move at all. His lack of awareness of that phone created a disaster for us because he left his seat before the final sheet of paper had dropped into the hopper. It caught fire under the gas jet.

That ended things. The building went up in flames. While the fire was not the biggest in the city's history, it was a front page story in San Diego's two dailies. It seemed that the entire San Diego fire department was at the site, and they poured tremendous amounts of water into the building. There was a surfeit of hoses, a number of them leaking. Both Susie and I were distraught with the way things went. The leaking hoses made us wonder about the competence of the fire department, and it seemed that a wall of water continued long after the fire was out. To put it mildly, the building and its contents were a complete mess. Susie busied herself taking files out of water-logged cabinets, but I remember sitting with Ed on the curb and suggesting we go play golf. And we did.

There were two reasons why golf seemed attractive. We had experienced a disaster, and any response to it was completely out of our control. I just wanted to get away from it. The other reason was more profound and had longer term consequence. I was disgusted with myself for having invested so heavily, and having really forced Susie to do so, in something so material as a printing plant. When I use the word, "invest," the feeling was not about money. It was that I had deluded myself that this was a good use of our own personal resources, that it would be a source of satisfaction to us, and that it would have a permanence in a world that is essentially impermanent. It may seem strange that such thoughts were running through my mind at such a tragic time. But they were. The reason is that I had learned an indelible lesson when I had visited a pile of rocks in Nuremberg, Germany, with the *maitre de* of the army officers' mess at which I ate at the time. Pointing to the rubble, he said, "There is my life. That is the restaurant to which I dedicated myself for many years." I remembered considering his anguish a statement of a sad misallocation of human energy. How silly it was to think that anything so temporary and material could provide meaning to a life!

Down deep, I felt the fire had liberated me. Without thinking much about it, I was following the pattern of the German *maitre de*. God knows how long Susie and I would have slaved away in that printing plant, perhaps a lifetime. One way or other, I had the premonition that we would have ended up with the same sense of disappointment as my German friend. Thus going off to play golf reflected contradictory emotions, frustration because of the inability to influence events and joy because I had been released from a wrong-headed passage through life.

Some verification of the importance of the release was a picture that appeared in the advertisement of an insurance company very shortly after the fire. It showed me receiving a check from the outfit that insured our equipment. I was positively haggard. My appearance was not the result of a couple of days of worry; it came from the long hours over many months that I spent trying to keep the business together.

Early in the morning after the fire, there was a knock on the door. To our surprise, an old friend, Hugo Fisher, said he needed to talk to us. Hugo, who went on to a distinguished career in California politics and service on the Superior Court bench, was in his last year of a local law school. "Have you ever heard of subrogation?" he asked. We had not. Indeed, we did not even know the word existed. To our horror, we learned that the insurer of the building would pay off the owner and then turn on us to secure reimbursement for the payment it had made. In the last analysis we were responsible for the fire. All legal tradition said that we were the ones who had to pay. That's subrogation. And, of course, I had refused to take out any property liability insurance.

Under the circumstances, Hugo advised that we take every step we could to keep any assets that remained from insurance company clutches. He said he would help us. The reality was, of course, that there wasn't much of anything. *Magazine San Diego* was unaffected; and our only physical assets were presses, a linotype, and trays of type, all of them water soaked and generally regarded as not salvageable. My recollection is that the insurance money we got went to pay off current bills. I don't think we had any real debts at the end, but we did not have any assets either. Hugo was in touch with the insurance company and was able to convince it that there was nothing to attach and no chance of getting money out of this turnip. Our only chance of salvaging something for ourselves was to do what most people thought was impossible, namely to restore the printing machinery to operating condition.[82]

Most of the large buildings that had housed a now dormant aircraft manufacturing facility in San Diego were then vacant. Space in these huge shells could be rented dirt cheap, and so we moved the printing machinery there. Then began literally months of clean up. Frances and Frank[10] were constantly bathed in kerosene. Saved was a Miehle press, which could be used for all kinds of job printing purposes; the linotype, and most of the trays of type. Linotypes have magazines that hold literally hundreds of brass pieces, each of them containing a letter. They had to be cleaned individually. Much to everyone's surprise, we did create a functioning print shop, not large but with all the necessary pieces. In fact, Ed and Frank[10] were able to compose at least a couple of issues of *Magazine San Diego* in this setting.

An asset of some value had, in effect, been created. The next goal was to sell it, as Frank[10] was still very much aware of his Nuremberg experience. Somehow an

---

[82] *Loc. cit.*

old acquaintance learned that things were up and running. He had grown up in a printing environment, his father having had a shop in San Diego. After the war the friend had gotten into housing construction and had prospered for a few years. But the recession of 1948-49 had essentially destroyed him financially; and his lone asset was the equity in a new house he had not been able to sell. He proposed that we trade. Without much haggling, a deal was struck; and then the Sherwoods' lone asset was a house in the relatively up-scale suburb of Loma Portal, worth, it turned out, about $15,000.

While the Sherwoods were disposing of the printing equipment, Ed also engineered an arrangement whereby the Sherwoods would sell their interest in *Magazine San Diego* to mutual friends, Charles and Blessing Muehling. Little money was exchanged for the half because, frankly, the magazine did not have much value at the time. In fact, it was a liability, not yet old enough to turn a profit. The great gain for the Sherwoods was that they were freed of a burden to support an investment that would need more cash.

By the early summer of 1949 and the sale of the Loma Portal property, it was possible to contemplate next moves. The Sherwoods now had $15,000 in the bank. Frank[10] wrote about this time about next steps:

> I have to confess that the middle of 1949 was a real downer for me. San Diego in those days was really the end of the line, made more so by its extreme recession. Like many other members of the "Greatest Generation," I did not have expectations of major success in life. Ed and I had lived on the dream of operating a major newspaper for roughly 10 years, and now that aspiration had vanished for both financial and personal reasons. There was really nothing to replace it. I was a child of the Depression; we just did not think there were all kinds of good things out there. Some illustration of how I was anticipating the construction of my life is to be seen in my thinking that I should go to San Diego State, get an education credential, and teach shop subjects. That would build on the skill I had developed on my own as a printer.
>
> The only other possibility I considered was to postpone the day of settling on the next employment step by returning to a university for a PhD. I had no idea what I might do with it, but the fact that my father had one seemed fairly compelling. I wrote about the possibility in my Army letters to my mother; but again it was framed as something "nice to do."
>
> It was at about this point in a somber period that the marvelous Susie intervened. She simply informed me that she was not about to become the wife of a

shop teacher. It was not a matter of hostility toward shop teachers. It was that I had more potential than that. I had a wife who believed in me.

It was Susie who pushed for the PhD option. She insisted that the graduate education was doable, and it could lead to enhanced possibilities. She was right about its being doable. One of the greatest pieces of legislation every enacted in the United States was then in full force, the GI Bill of Rights. It was designed to enable returning soldiers to pursue educational objectives at government expense. It was a tremendous gift to the returning veterans. When I was at the Federal Executive Institute, I heard many senior executives detail how the GI bill had made it possible for young, impecunious men to get a university education and go on to careers that otherwise would have been foreclosed to them. I resonated with all those tales because mine was the same. Had it not been for the GI bill, Susie and I could never have contemplated my obtaining a PhD. All that followed would never have occurred. Government has been very good to me, and it has repaid me amply for the time I spent in its service.[83]

The Move to Los Angeles

In August, 1949, Frances and Frank[10] departed San Diego, each with admissions to universities in Los Angeles in hand. Frances was headed for the University of California at Los Angeles (UCLA), where she would be able to complete her major in English in an academic year. Frank[10] was bound for UCLA's cross-town rival, the private University of Southern California, where he would matriculate for a master's degree in Public Administration and a PhD in Political Science. Economically, the GI Bill was the basic source of support. It paid all Frank[10]'s college bills, plus a monthly stipend of about $150 per month. There was no tuition but only fees at UCLA, and so Frances' expenses were mostly out-of-pocket ones.

The money from the sale of the house in San Diego, $15,000, provided the cash cushion, and Frank[10] rather quickly secured part-time work as a printer at SC's University Press.[84]

---

[83] *Loc. cit.*

[84] See Frank P. Sherwood, *Reflections on Public Administration Education.* (Tallahassee, Fl., 1992, processed, a Jerry Collins Eminent Scholar Publication), 22 pages. The first section, "On Being a Student," provides detail on Frank[10]'s graduation education at the University of Southern California, pgs. 1-8. The second section, "On Being a Teacher," covers his experience as a professor of Public Administration, pgs. 9-22.

Frances received her B.A. degree at UCLA's Hollywood Bowl commencement exercises in June, 1950. Ralph Bunche, himself a UCLA graduate and at the time a prominent figure in the United Nations, was the speaker. Shortly thereafter, she took a position as a clerk in the Pacific Coast Borax Company in downtown Los Angeles. Her new job was reflective of the times. Even with a college degree, Frances' only employment opportunity was as a clerk. For the young couple, however, it was a real step forward. Family finances were greatly improved, and a move was soon made to a modern apartment in Santa Monica, about a block from the beach.

Frank[10] also got a degree in 1950. During the summer he completed his thesis for the Master of Science in Public Administration and was awarded the degree formally in August. There remained another year of course work in Political Science. Early in 1951 he was given an opportunity to teach an extension class in Public Administration, thus inaugurating a long career in the field. Having negotiated that tryout in the classroom, Frank[10] was offered a full-time, tenure-earning position as a Visiting Assistant Professor, commencing in the fall, 1951, with a salary of $4000 per academic year. The "visiting" was to be removed when he had received his PhD in Political Science.

Launched on a career with high stability and modest economic prospects, Frances and Frank[10] felt their future was relatively secure. As a result, they took part of their cash cushion and bought a Santa Monica lot ($1500) on which they built a small, two-bedroom house. Married three years, they were poised to start a family. It was also important that Frank[10] had prevailed on his mother, Mildred, to move to Los Angeles. She bought a large two-story house in central Los Angeles, where some work had already been done on developing it into apartments. For the next two years, Frank[10] spent every spare moment on construction activity. At the end, five apartments were created; and they became an important source of income for Mildred.

It was about 15 months after they had moved into their house in Santa Monica that Jeffrey[11] Kirk Sherwood arrived, on January 16, 1953 to be exact. His sister, Robin[11] Ann Sherwood, followed 18 months later, on June 25, 1954. Both were born in the Santa Monica Hospital. Thus, by mid-1954, the 10th generation Sherwood family was formed. For the next 20 years the Sherwood family life revolved around the parents and their two offspring.

As has already been indicated, it is important that this history capture as much of the dynamic life of its various characters as possible. For that reason, what several of the principal characters have written about the two decades in two volumes, one recognizing the 40th birthday of Jeffrey[11] and the other that of Robin[11], constitute our means of reporting what really happened in the family. The three reporters are Frances, who, as the mother, saw more of family life that anyone else; Jeffrey[11], who tells about events involving his sister; and Robin[11], whose reporting focuses on her brother. Frances, of course, has the 360 degree perspective.

Vignettes That Cover 20 Years of Family Life

Pre-school years

> <u>Jeff on Robin</u>: "Our early years are sort of a fog…I have no recollection of you when we lived on Victor [1957-61], except that there was a girl across the street, possibly named Rachel, who you would play with sometimes. Frank kept his old Austin in the backyard and what was really remarkable about it was that it had flags which stuck out of its side in lieu of turn signals. You and I played in that car all the time. There was plenty of adventure on Victor with Grandma's cottage, the tree house, and that shed near the rose bushes. We had a name for it which I have since forgotten, but it was a dangerous place. And I always believed that behind us lived an old woman with snakes, crocodiles, and all sorts of scary animals.
>
> "I have better memories of our trip to South America…[1960] It was a great expedition for us, you drank Orange Crush at virtually every meal and I always had Coke, even at dinner! And on street corners people would rub my fuzzy little head while you were the little American darling. We had some horrendous plane trips, with Frank usually adding a little suspense by disappearing just before they would finish boarding."
>
> <u>Robin on Jeff</u>: "It would be nice if I could recollect exactly when I became aware of you. But I can't so I'll have to start around the advanced age of 6…I really don't even remember you at age 6 that well. But I do remember our house on Victor and the trip to South America, and I am sure you fit in there somewhere. Mainly we fought a lot. Or did that come later? Or did it go on all the time?
>
> <u>Frances on Jeff</u>: "His travel history began at an early age. Before walking he was flying. The first was only a flight from Los Angeles to San Diego and back, but it was his Mom's second flight so we were adventuring together…While on a one week trip to San Diego after Robin was born, we found that Jeff had taken a great dislike to any bed but his own. After three nights without sleep, we packed up and went home.
>
> "We were pushed to the purchase of a travel trailer in order to get some arrangement to enable us to journey to Estes Park, Colorado, where Frank was to spend two weeks in a special program. With two children in diapers, we set off across the desert in our Plymouth, pulling our 15-foot trailer. Approaching the western slopes of the Rockies, we aimed for Trail Ridge Road which would lead us to Estes Park. We arrived late one night on the outskirts of Steamboat Springs. We tried to find a quiet spot off the road

[no state parks around] and felt we succeeded. Early the next morning we peered out the window to see where we had landed. The first thing we saw was a big sign, 'No Dead Horses'! We were in the town dump!

"A highlight of the trip was…when we camped in the National Park campground at the South Rim of the Grand Canyon…and watched deer come right into the camp area. Jeff was so excited he could hardly sleep, wanting to watch out the window for more deer.

"Pets came and went. After Gus [the dog Frank had brought from Germany] was killed under the wheels of a truck and my beloved Cocker Spaniel, Teufel, died, we settled on Siamese cats. One was selected as a Christmas present in 1954—that was cross-eyed Gigi. Then the Armers gave us one they did not like—that was Zaza. The two of them kept us busy along with the Storm's cocker spaniel who boarded with us while the family was in Iran for two years. Next, we had two beagles, Gretchen and Tippy. They came to bad ends. Both ran away. Our dear old Gigi was lost in the Baldwin Hills flood when the Storm's house was washed away. Marge Shirley gave us a new Siamese, Samba, who later delivered Cinza to us. And we had Gretchen II, a German Shepherd, presented by a vet who had patched her and needed a home for her. She ran away and was last seen chasing rabbits on the runway at LA International Airport. We believe she was later adopted by a TWA crew member."

<u>Frances on Robin</u>: "The worst moment I recall was when we went to the beach in Ocean Park and you became frightened of something (the crowds maybe) and took off leaving your parents frantically searching in all directions. Nothing has ever frightened me so much. Thank Heavens I wasn't there when Frank lost you at the Sheriff's Rodeo in the Los Angeles Coliseum and found you riding around on the shoulders of a Deputy Sheriff…

"Back on Chesapeake street (1954-57) we got along fine, overcoming such obstacles as milk allergy, heat rash, the distractions of two Siamese cats, and a mildly jealous older brother. Your efforts to keep up with that brother were a wonder to all of us. Sometimes you got yourself into positions from which you didn't know how to escape…

"…After we moved to Inglewood (Victor 1957-61), you started kindergarten at Highland School. On one of your first days there you came home in tears, right after being deposited there. 'They closed the door, Mommy!' We went back and found our way through the front door, and all was well. It was a great help to have a house so close to the school—a few steps to the corner and one could see the front of the school. Until junior high days, we were never more than two or three blocks from school.

"...Christmases were always big celebrations—your Dad's family went in for generous holidays, and we kept up the tradition. Aunt Betty and your Grandmother Mildred were always there, and often my mother. Lots of packages and good times. One year I recalled Ed and Gloria Self sent a cardboard General Store (some assembly required). Your Dad nearly went out of his mind figuring out how to set it up, but there were few toys that you and Jeff enjoyed so much as that one. And do you remember Hula Hoops? In 1957 we had a different kind of holiday—your Dad was in Iran—and his packages had to come from Marshall Field's in Chicago, ordered by catalog."

Pre-High School Years

<u>Frances on Jeff</u>: "When we went back to live in Rio de Janeiro (1962), we decided to go by boat in order to ship our household effects at the same time, and thus avoid months without them. It was a big experience for Jeff—all of the natural gregariousness and charm came into full play. He knew virtually every passenger, and for sure every steward on the *S.S. Del Sud*. He had a grand time. Lifeboat drills were even fun. The night before our 17-day voyage ended in Rio, he cried because he didn't want to leave the ship and all his friends."

<u>Frances on Robin</u>: "There were 34 missionaries on that boat [the *Del Sud*], all going to convert the Brazilians. They had lots of children, and one little girl took a shine to Frank, climbing on his lap at every opportunity. At this Robin took umbrage, shoving her off and exclaiming, 'He's my Daddy!' And when Frank was chosen to be King Neptune for the crossing of the Equator, Robin and Jeff, dressed in satin costumes, were the pages.

"School was an adjustment for you, I know, for they were already doing cursive writing and you worried about that, and you worried about learning Portuguese. Our chauffeur was patient, calm, and avuncular. He had no children, but he had a kind heart and was very careful of you and Jeff. When you were so terribly ill with fever, he asked to see you. When I took him up to our room, where we had positioned you directly under our only air conditioner, he told me he was so glad we didn't have it on. That would be very bad, he said. He was a superstitious, uneducated man, but he was the closest thing to a nanny we ever had.

Mercedes, our cook, was another memorable character, thief though she was. Ingratiating and sympathetic, she taught us all to samba as Carnival approached. And what better teacher than a Bahiana? She worked especially hard to teach Frank and get us equipped for the big dances to come. There were even children's Samba parties. I don't think you went to any of these, being a bit young and reluctant to try your dancing but we surely watched a lot of it."

Jeff on Brazil: "And then of course we lived in Brazil, where you and I had one of the immortal camp experiences. It must say something about Brian Jones that he wanted to stay another week. I am not sure we ever wanted to see our parents so desperately! One of our favorite places in Brazil was Paquita, the island [in Guanabara Bay] with no cars. It was great because it reduced grownups to riding bicycles. You will recall that we belonged to three clubs down there. I never understood why we belonged to the Yacht Club because we never had a boat. It had a big pool, though, and I remember two girls with green hair—they swam so much, the chlorine turned their hair green. But mostly you and I had steak and fries at the Paisandu Club. I think by then you had converted from Orange Crush to Coca-Cola.

"We went to Escola Americana, and I quickly moved up through Portuguese class to 'advanced' while you stayed in 'beginner' the whole time, even though your Portuguese was just as good as mine. Perhaps that was just a little Brazilian sexism, a problem I am sure they have long since corrected."

Robin on Brazil. "Brazil is perhaps where my memory gets sharper. Learning Portuguese seemed to be a snap for you, and I was irritated that you progressed to the higher Portuguese classes faster than I did.

Robin on the European Trip after Brazil [1963-64]: "Most of all I remember our good times and fighting on the trip home through Europe. In the back of the VW, we bugged the hell out of each other. We planted a tree in Sherwood forest, got violently ill in Istanbul, rode camels in Egypt, climbed up in the tombs and were mystified by the death of JFK."

Jeff on the trip: "Of course, we came home through Europe and there was the apocryphal moment, when, riding in our new Volkswagon, we nearly drove off the edge of the Alps. But that hardly stopped you and me from drawing lines in the backseat and arguing about who should be in the front seat...But your moment came at Christmas time in London, which I remember to be quite cold and miserable, when you were adamant we had to have a Christmas tree. And so we purchased one at Woolworth's, I believe...Afterwards you wanted to make a pilgrimage to Sherwood Forest for a ritual planting of this rather forlorn and thoroughly dead sapling. And so we did, though finding a piece of forest proved challenging."

Frances on the trip: Robin has mentioned the trip home through Europe and the Middle East. In Athens Jeff, in characteristic fashion, climbed into the front seat of the cab to try to talk to the driver. The driver began to shout at us in a hostile manner, and we could not communicate a word except our destination. Finally, we got out of the cab and stood looking at him. It turned out that by law, no one could ride in the front seat. Many memories of Jeff on that trip—learning a word or two here and there of Arabic, Turkish, French, and so on."

Frances on life in California: "Jeff progressed through Airport Junior High School with a plan. He was going to be student body president, and he carefully navigated all the intricate steps that were laid out for that important job. He had fun doing it, I think, and those were some pretty good years for him. Though he didn't grow as tall as he would have liked, his skills grew apace. The big disappointment came at graduation when the Principal would not let him prepare his own speech. It was a blow and one we had never anticipated. Our experiences had been so different—there was more trust in our day.

We drove to Mt. Pinos in our first Volkswagon, about 100 miles north of Los Angeles.

"One thing about Jeff and Robin that has always pleased their parents is their willingness, within reason, to relate in an interested and generally pleasant way to our many friends. Maybe we pushed this, but I prefer to think it happened because we all had a lot of good experiences and fun **together**. Those skiing trips, the picnics, train trips, endless lunches and dinner with all sorts of folks left some good feelings.

"....The Berkovs...had a warm spot for [Robin]. When she later went to Geneva to study French at the university there, it was their benevolent oversight that made us feel comfortable leaving our 17-year-old so far from home."

Jeff on California: "...We plowed on with school and enjoyed the swimming pool immensely. Not only was the house large [Bradna], but the backyard was a jungle with a myriad of hiding places. Eventually it was on to junior high school, and I remember the horrible car pool I had to endure. I can only remember the jockey's mother who was morbidly obese, to use a medical term, and smelled horrifically of hair oil. I do believe that she was the inspiration for the cartoon character of Ursula, the Sea Witch, in *Little Mermaid*."

Robin on California: "...Ah, that was a great house [Bradna]. It seems larger than any house I've ever lived in since. We were both downstairs, your [Jeff's] room was dark, without a lot of light, at the foot of the stairs. I think I got a better deal, in terms of rooms...We had great fun with the slot cars that Frank put together for us. (Of course, I had one too). And we watched Star Trek up in the TV room, and peered out the

View Room to the pool and the backyard below. As long as I live, I doubt I will forget that stupid View Room, for the life of me I don't know why. (Maybe I remember it because that is where the Christmas tree went.)"

"We left California, all its good skiing, smog and beaches for the rolling hills of Virginia."

Virginia-High School and College

Robin on living in Key West: "We played pool, you much better than I, but you were kind enough to let me beat you. We fought the day to day battles of being adolescents, and about this time we decided we really were on the same side. The battle was no longer between us; we figured it would be more fun to get along. I suppose that was the beginning of our lifelong friendship.

"I can't let the Bolling Brook [we lived on Bolling Brook ave. in Key West, Charlottesville] period go by without a comment on your room, again downstairs and a bit dark. It was quite removed from the rest of the house, and it definitely was not a place one would go unless one really had to. It was in a constant state of mess. You tried to grow a beard, of sorts, and we all began to think that you might be losing your hair.

Robin[11] faces away from the beautiful countryside at Obidos, Portugal, 1963

"I guess that you had a good time in high school and did not work too hard. You certainly did not seem worried about what you were going to do with your life and appeared to be dead set on enjoying yourself while you figured it out.

"After Albemarle high school you went to Idaho for a summer of fire fighting...I went to Spain, Portugal and Switzerland...At the end of the summer, it was on to the University of Virginia; but most of your buddies at Albermarle High also went there, so you weren't lonely. To help you out, I used your Austin Healy to pick up and deliver your laundry. One day on the 250 bypass I lost your muffler in the road. I stopped to pick it up but had no place to put it, so I threw it in the bushes."

Jeff on living in Key West: "I certainly have a number of fond memories of our time in Charlottesville, especially when you and I became closer friends. To the best of my recollection, your first date was with Steve Ashby, and he took you to the Albemarle prom. I was certainly pleased that he took you, although I confess I had higher hopes for you...

"When I left for college, you got the use of my Austin Healy, and there you were, driving a convertible to school every day. That must have seemed like a pretty good deal, except for those days when the exhaust pipe and assembly would fall off. I remember your calling me at the dorm one time, and I had to come out and put the damn thing back on. All in all, though, I remember being fairly pleased that I could do such a good thing for my sister."

College (1972-76)

Robin: "I graduated from Albemarle and decided to go to Colby College…Frank and Susie were still driving that 1964 Chevrolet Impala. Amazed? Frank's colleagues were thinking of buying him a new car, they were so embarrassed. You drove with all of us to Maine, to drop me off, I guess you were naturally curious and were perhaps slowly coming to the realization that UVa wasn't all you thought it would be. You were an extremely kind and considerate brother to come with me, but even more important, you lent me your entire stereo system and most of your records. I can still remember your setting it up for me in my small room in Small Hall. You surely did not want me going to some fancy New England school without the right tunes. You cared.

"Your interest in Colby was not completely satisfied with that one visit because you organized the great 'Virginia comes to Maine' trip in the winter 1973. This was the trip in which you, Tom, V, Frank and Linda traveled *en masse* to Colby. You all went skiing, fought with Linda, and lined the window sills of the dorm with Dawsons."

Jeff: "The following year marked a new chapter in our lives when we both were in college. In the fall, an entourage of Albemarle Patriots descended upon quiet, unsuspecting Colby College and a nice freshman girl. These rough southern types invaded a girls' dorm, sleeping anywhere, and keeping security forces busy, while lining the windows outside the dorm with 16 oz. bottles of Dawsons' lager beer, a rough New England swill that cost 99 cents for six bottles. These ruffians included your brother, a ringleader, Studebaker Romer, V the Latvian pimp, Frank 'Give me a Dawsons' Thornton and Linda 'Born in Sin' Seaborn. And they met your next significant boy friend, Dash Riprock, aka Caveman, aka California Bob. Now Dash was a pretty nice guy, and we all liked him quite a bit. And he was responsible for one of your memorable names—Cavewoman. In my time with you at Colby, there were a few memorable cartoons drawn by some of Dash's dormitory neighbors about Caveman and Cavewoman."

Robin: "When you applied to several schools to transfer, I can remember talking to you on the phone about the prospects at Colby. They didn't look good. I called the Admissions people to see what being on the waiting list really meant, and they told me. It meant that maybe you'd get in the day before school started if someone didn't show up at the last moment. I told them thanks a lot but my brother had other offers and that was too much of a gamble. So I delivered the disappointing news to you, only to find out about an hour later that the Admissions people totally reversed themselves and let you in unconditionally. We now know what they were thinking…If we get two kids from the same family to graduate…We'll surely get *beaucoup* bucks when they are alumni!"

It seems appropriate to conclude this section with a report on another, major part of Sherwood family life: the 15 acre farm in Banco, Virginia, which was purchased in 1975 (when both kids were in college) and sold in 1981. Robin has succinctly detailed the way in which this property proved unforgettable for all of us. She wrote:

> While I was away, Banco was acquired, which began the great Madison County Era. You [Jeff] and Tom started the Great Beers of America party, which eventually led to your current state of marital bliss.[Jeff met wife Jae at one of the parties.] I think it was on a trip to Chicago that in search of new and better beers, you loaded your suitcase with some Heilmann's *Special Export* and other Midwestern brews. Unfortunately, they broke and you came home dripping beer all over. We voted Heilmann's the best beer at least once but also enjoyed Strohs and Rolling Rock, and saved Red White and Blue for the end of the party. We tried inviting Dan Rather (I think) or was it Charles Kuralt, explaining that it was truly a celebration of AMERICAN BEER, second to none. I should also note, especially for Jae's benefit since in later years I think some of this was lost, you were dubbed Toastmaster of the Shenandoah Chapter of the Benevolent and Protective Order of the Beer Drinkers of America (or BPOBDA, as it is affectionately known).

A More Systematic Summary of Sherwood Family Events During 1953-1976

The Sherwood family remained in Los Angeles for nearly 20 years, from 1949 to 1968. Throughout that period, Frank[10] was closely tied to the University of Southern California's School of Public Administration. In 1957 he was promoted to full professor and was playing a leading role in its activities. Not only was the School the focus of his professional activities, but it was also the center of the family's social life. To a remarkable degree the relatively small faculty of the School had a concentration of professors whose ages differed by very few years. Indeed, four [and they constituted a group who were particularly close] were born within a year of each other. Further, the 10 children of Richard and Myra

Gable, Bruce and Harriet Storm, David and Marge Shirley, and Frank[10] and Frances Sherwood were of remarkably similar ages.

While the four families had somewhat greater contact, the entire School of Public Administration constituted a social group. They formed the core of a network that extended not only to other parts of the university but to a considerable portion of the governmental community. The Sherwoods had a very active social life, one in which Jeff[11] and Robin[11] were active participants.[85]

Robin[11] on the beach at Nazare, a picturesque fishing village in Portugal. 1963

The involvement of the USC School of Public Administration in major technical assistance efforts in Public Administration in the post-World War II period, largely financed by the U.S. government, made it possible for Frank[10] to take the family to South America on two different occasions, the second for a period of 17 months. Though the children were young, these two trips were major events for the entire family, as is to be seen in the excerpts from reports in the 40-year books. In the summer, 1960, the family toured South America, including Peru, Chile, Uruguay, and Argentina, leaving Frank[10] in Brazil to audit the progress of a major technical assistance project begun two years earlier. In the summer, 1962, Frank[10] returned with his family to Rio de Janeiro to serve as chief of the technical assistance project. A month tour of Europe and the Near East followed the assignment in Brazil, with the family arriving back in Los Angeles in January, 1964.

In the summer, 1967, Frank[10] was invited to participate in a month-long seminar at the University of North Carolina. The seminar provided an opportunity for the family to tour the East Coast, and the itinerary included New England and the Middle Atlantic states, prior to settling for a month in Chapel Hill, North Carolina. Of special significance was a visit to the University of Virginia in

---

[85] For a sense of the social life of the Sherwoods in the 1950's see Frank P. Sherwood, *Comparing the 90s with the 50s: A Memoir Inspired by the Film, "Pleasantville"* (Tallahassee, Florida: December, 1998), processed, 29pgs.

Charlottesville, Virginia. At the time it seemed to be simply a sightseeing venture, but events the next year gave it particular importance.

Changes began with a phone call to Frank[10] in April, 1968 from John W. Macy, Jr., the Chairman of the U.S. Civil Service Commission and President Lyndon Johnson's Special Assistant for Personnel. Macy asked Frank[10] whether he would be interested in becoming the director of a proposed new senior staff college for the Federal government, named the Federal Executive Institute. Frank[10], who had served as Director of the SC School of Public Administration for less than a year, told Macy the timing was wrong, that he could not leave the School after such short service as its leader. Macy said he understood the situation but asked for one concession. Would Frank[10] wait 24 hours before giving him a final answer? Macy wanted to be sure his proposal had been given careful consideration.

When he reported to Frances that night on the day's events, Frank[10] included the conversation with Macy. He finished, "Of course, I told John I had to refuse." Frances exclaimed, "You what?" She believed that Frank[10] had some interest in the job but did not feel free to think about it. Frances pointed out that Frank[10] had given 17 years of service to the university and should now have earned the right at least to consider another career opportunity.

The upshot was that Frank[10] called Macy the next day and agreed to go to Washington to discuss the position. It took very little time for Frank[10] to sense the exciting challenge of the Federal Executive Institute. He accepted the job, subject to family approval. When he got home, the four in the family took a vote. There was unanimous agreement to move to Charlottesville, and the agreement by Jeff[11] and Robin[11] may have been eased because they had seen the place to which they were going a year earlier.

The five years in Charlottesville, from 1968 to 1973, were ones that had great significance in the family. Jeffrey[11] arrived in Charlottesville as a high school sophomore and was a sophomore at the University of Virginia at the end of the period. Robin[11] was still in Junior High School in 1973 and had finished her first year at Colby College when Frank[10]'s resignation as Director of the Federal Executive Institute took effect. The FEI had been every bit the challenge that Frank[10] had anticipated,[86] and Frances devoted many of her energies to leadership roles in the League of Women Voters, which was particularly strong in Charlottesville.

---

[86] For a more general look at some of the problems and issues at the Federal Executive Institute, see Frank P. Sherwood, *Selected Papers: Executive Development at the Federal Executive Institute.* Charlottesvilllle, Va.: U.S. Civil Service Commission, Federal Executive Institute, 1971) 86 p.

With the departure of the two children for college [Jeffrey[11] joined Robin[11] at Colby College in the Fall, 1973], mother Frances was feeling very much alone. She did not at all enjoy the "empty nest," and she felt a strong imperative to move into the workplace. But the year was 1973, and it had been more than 20 years since Frances had worked. The one person who knew and fully appreciated her talents was her husband, Frank[10]. He felt strongly the two had to be associated in whatever new undertaking there was.

The faculty at the School of Public Administration [from which Frank[10] had been on leave throughout his service at the FEI] was anxious for him to return to Los Angeles. Frank[10], however, felt that he had a rich knowledge of the Federal government and that it needed to be put to further use. After considerable discussion, it was decided that Frank[10] should launch a new USC program in Washington, D.C., the Washington Public Affairs Center. To this possibility, Frank[10] added only one condition: Frances would be the new program's Administrative Officer.

The final decision to establish the Center had to be made by the University's Vice President and Provost, Zohrab Kaprelian, whom Assistant Dean Ross Clayton and Frank[10] visited for a wrap-up meeting. Things went along easily; and, at the end, Dean Clayton said, "There is one thing I want to make clear. Frank's acceptance of this job carries one crucial condition. His wife has to be the administrative officer. To this obvious instance of nepotism, Kaprelian responded, "This is what is great about the private university! We can rise above principle!" He went on to observe that Frank[10]'s wife would not be leaving at 5 p.m.

Frank[10] spent an exciting and productive three years as Director of the WPAC, stepping down because he felt the pace was too much for him [he was 55].[87] Frances, very much at the center of the operation, stayed on as Student Affairs officer for another year, at which time the two returned to Charlottesville, Virginia. Frank[10] went to the Federal Executive Institute as a faculty member.

There was one particular event in the Washington experience that will always have a special place in the family memory. It was Christmas, 1973, when the United States was suffering its worst gas shortage. Both children were then at Colby and were flying to the Washington National Airport just before Christmas. The rainfall was heavy as the parents drove on the George Washington Parkway to meet them. Suddenly there was a lake of water through which the car sought to navigate. It did not. It had drowned and would not start. Exactly how events

---

[87] For the full account of the Washington Public Affairs Center, see Frank P. Sherwood, *The Beginning and the End of the Washington Public Affairs Center.* (Reston, Va., 2001), processed.

unfolded from this point is lost to time, but the fact was that the car would not be repaired for days. Somehow, the parents got to the airport, found their two kids, and got themselves back to their fourth floor walk-up on New Hampshire Ave. near Dupont Circle.

The four basically found themselves without transportation for the holidays. Taxicabs were impossible to get. The bus system was woefully inadequate. And so walking was the only viable option. That is what the four did. They walked—to do their Christmas shopping at Hecht's and Woodward and Lothrop, to the Kennedy Center to see the classic movie, "Palm Beach Story," to eat at various restaurants, and otherwise to have a good time. All remembered it as one of the most joyous Christmases they had ever had.

That Christmas, 1973, was in many ways the celebration of the end. Both Jeffrey[11] and Robin[11] were well established in college by that time and were certainly finding that they had their own lives to live. There were times when they resided with their parents for relatively short periods, but they probably never again thought of the family home as a permanent address.

The 10th Generation of Sherwoods from 1977 to 2006 (The Present)

Frank[10] remained on the faculty of the Federal Executive Institute for five years, from 1977 to 1982. Frances once again assumed the presidency of the League of Women Voters and then decided to move in an entirely different direction. She became a painter. Over the years she has received considerable recognition and is a Signature member of the Florida Watercolor Society and the Texas Watercolor Society.

The departure from the FEI in 1982 was accompanied by an offer to Frank[10] from the College of Social Sciences at the Florida State University to become Professor and Chair of the Department of Public Administration. Frank[10] accepted and was Chair for five years from 1982 to 1987 and served on the faculty for 13 years, retiring in 1995. He was named Jerry Collins Eminent Scholar in Public Administration in 1991 and retained that designation until his retirement. Later, in 2005, a chair in his name was created.

A major event at Florida State University was the Sherwood Symposium on Administrative Change, organized by George Frederickson of the University of Kansas and a former student, and Richard Chackerian, of FSU. It was planned to operate two days, November 20 and 21, 1992, but really spread out over four days. About 100 former students, colleagues and friends assembled for the event. Five came from Brazil, which was the most heavily represented foreign country, but there were also former students from Saudi Arabia and Pakistan.

In 1983 Frances and Frank[10] built a new house in Tallahassee, an undertaking in which they invested substantial effort. The house was located on an acre of land and also had a swimming pool and a tennis court. When Frances' mother, Verna, died in August 2000, they quickly decided they should sell the property and move near at least one of their two children. Later in 2000, they bought a townhouse in Reston, Virginia, near the Great Falls home of Jeffrey[11]. In that same year they also acquired a small house in Tallahassee, with the idea that they would spend their winters there. They sold their large house in Tallahassee in the spring, 2001.

Since that time Frances and Frank[10] have had two residences, spending part of the year in Virginia and part in Florida. They have continued to live in Wilmington, Vermont, in July and August, in the house the family bought in 1993.

Jeffrey[11] graduated from Colby College in 1975 with a BA in English. He received his JD from Stanford University in 1989 and immediately began the practice of law in Richmond, Virginia. He married Jae Anne Seward on April 5, 1980, and they had three children: Evan MacKinlay, born October 4, 1984; Lindsay Beckwith, April 2, 1986; and Amanda Persons, November 22, 1989. Jeffrey[11] is a partner in the law firm of Aiken, Gump, Strauss, Hauer and Feld in Washington, D.C.

Robin[11] graduated from Colby College in 1976 with a BA in East Asian Studies, spending her junior year at the prestigious Waseda University in Japan. She received her MBA from the Wharton School at the University of Pennsylvania in 1981 and began a career in business. She married Andrew M. Ziolkowski on May 14, 1983, and they had two children: Emily Ann, born March 24, 1986; and Sonya Sherwood, December 14, 1987. Robin[11] is associated with HTG Associates in New Canaan, Connecticut, as a Certified Financial Planner.

The members of the 11th and 12th generations of this branch of the Sherwood family still have much of their lives to live. They do not yet belong in a history of the family, and so a more detailed account of their lives will await another day.

The Sherwood family-the ones who go by the name of Sherwood, that is. From left, Grandfather Frank[10], Granddaughter Lindsay[12], Grandson Evan[12], Granddaughter Amanda12, Mother Jae, Grandmother Frances, and son Jeff[11]. Informal picture in front of family fireplace.

A different name, Ziolkowski, but still Sherwoods. Robin[11] still uses her maiden name professionally, but the rest are Ziolkowskis. Husband Andy, with granddaughters Sonya[12] (at left) and Emily[12]. They were on a Carribean cruise.

FAMILY GROUP SHEET
Husband: Frank[10] Persons Sherwood
Born 11 October 1920 in Brunswick, Georgia
Married 14 February 1948 Laguna Beach, California
Father Clarence MacKinlay Sherwood
Mother Mildred Kirk Persons
Wife: Frances Howell
Born 26 November 1926 in Corsicana, Texas
Father John Virgil Howell
Mother Verna C. Robinson
CHILDREN
1 Jeffrey Kirk Sherwood
Born 16 January 1953 in Santa Monica, California
2 Robin Ann Sherwood
Born 25 June 1954 in Santa Monica, California

FAMILY GROUP SHEET
Husband: Jeffrey Kirk Sherwood
Born 16 January 1953 in Santa Monica, Calif.
Married 05 April 1980 Cambridge, Maryland
Father Frank[10] Persons Sherwood
Mother Frances Howell
Wife: Jae Anne Seward
Born 04 August 1957 in Grand Rapids, Mich.
Father James Hodson Seward
Mother Marilyn A. Rudjinski
CHILDREN
1 Evan MacKinlay Sherwood
Born 04 October 1984 in Washington, D.C.
2 Lindsay Beckwith Sherwood
Born 02 April 1986 in Washington, D.C.
3 Amanda Persons Sherwood
Born 22 November 1989 in Washington D.C.

FAMILY GROUP SHEET
Husband: Andrew Mark Ziolkowski
Born 30 March 1953 in Preston, England
Married 14 May 1983 in Middlebury, Conn.
Father: Klemens Ziolkowski
Mother: Irene Pall
Wife: Robin Ann Sherwood
Born 25 June 1954 in Santa Monica, Calif.
Father Frank[10] Persons Sherwood
Mother Frances Howell
CHILDREN
1 Emily Ann Ziolkowski
Born 24 March 1986 in Danbury, Conn.
2 Sonya Sherwood Ziolkowski
Born 14 December 1987 in Norwalk, Conn.

APPENDIX ONE

The Widowhood of Mildred Persons Sherwood

by Frank[10] Persons Sherwood

This is a very difficult part of this book to write. My mother's life with my father was a totally blissful one. But it lasted such a short time. Both of them deserved better. There is a sadness that accompanies death, but there is nothing more that can be written about my father. He was gone.

Mildred, on the other hand, lived into old age. She was nearly 83 when she passed away.

From my perspective, hers was a very sad life. In writing that, however, I have to emphasize that is my view. Mildred did not dwell on the inequities of life. While she grieved for my father, she also found great pleasure in her only son. She really did try to make the best of things; and, as I have written earlier, she never did try to unload the sadness she must have felt on me.

Her love for Clarence[9] was so profound that she never seemed to have an interest in developing a relationship with another man. That was too bad because she was quite a good-looking woman, fun-loving, and with a lot of enthusiasm and energy for things in general. There was one man, a Mr. Perry, who had a Stutz Bearcat, who took an interest in her. They had a couple of dates, but I did not sense this was a big deal for her. I did not like him because he had hair growing out of his ears. Very unfortunately, it was I who told her she should forget him—which she did. I was about six at the time, and I was jealous. Though I doubt anything would have come of the relationship, I have regretted for many years that I said anything to her.

Aside from her son, the only other male companion in her life was Charles L. Turner. They had a close relationship for about 15 years, but it was totally platonic—a real friendship. Turner had a wife and four children, to whom he was deeply committed. There was emotion but distance in their association. While they were genuinely fond of each other, the distance was evident in the fact that she always called him, "Mr. Turner." In some ways, my mother always remained Victorian. Hers was a formal relationship, and therefore the reference had to be formal. In the course of this essay, Mr. Turner (and I always called him that—I could not bring myself even to call him C.L.) will appear numerous times. He was always there when help was needed.

Mostly, however, Mildred's story is about her continuing efforts to make a living and be a good mother to her son. The two are related but also separate. She was a failure economically and an absolute success maternally.

As has been reported earlier, she arrived from Brunswick with the full intent that she would live an independent life, close to, but not in the bosom of, her family. Her first move was to buy a couple of pieces of real estate, and we moved into part of a duplex at 27th and A streets in San Diego in 1924. It was from there that I began kindergarten at Brooklyn Elementary school in 1925. That was the year, too, that the station in Hillcrest was moved to a new location at 3311 El Cajon Blvd., in the

This does not really show the Mission Fernery, but the lath houses are observable. To the right was the newly built service station. The structure on the left became the Flower Pot.

northeastern part of San Diego. Bess and Kirk Persons had built a new station on the corner, which they had rented. The old station was not much of a building, but presumably it had enough value to justify moving it to the new site. It was there that Mildred undertook a new entrepreneurial venture. She had the idea that people were ready for a store that specialized in green plants, such as ferns. In order to provide a proper setting for the new enterprise, which was called the Mission Fernery, she built at least 75 feet of lath houses from the back of the old service station to the rear property line. It must have involved a substantial investment, and there was considerably more money needed to turn the old station into a proper store.

The only thing I really remember about the undertaking was mud. The soil there was called adobe, and it was known by everyone as extremely difficult. When it was wet, it clung to your feet. It was difficult to navigate in it. When it was dry, it was rock hard. In the lath house, it seemed that it was nearly always wet and damp. I do recall my mother working exceptionally hard, as she did in everything, but there was apparently no way to make this business a success. People cared a lot less about green plants than she thought. And 33rd and El Cajon Blvd. was then out in the sticks. The operation went bust in about two years, and I have no idea how big the loss on that was.

The collapse of the business in 1926 or 1927 coincided with the foreclosure on the houses she owned. We moved back to 25th street, where we stayed.

My next memory is her affiliation with the John Austin development company, which had impressive offices next to the Spreckles theater downtown on Broadway between second and third streets. The company was engaged in a major land development at Crown Point and later at Pacific Beach. What made the property attractive was the intention of the government to build a causeway that would reach across Mission Bay from its southern side to Crown Point, a relatively small peninsula jutting out in the bay, on the north. Pacific Beach, a vast expanse of land that reached to the Pacific ocean, lay further north. When mother worked with the Austin Co., the Crown Point lots were sold out and she concentrated on Pacific Beach.

She was engaged in this venture when times were good, and I have the impression that she at least made a living. It was during this time that, at my insistence, she enrolled me for the summer session at the San Diego Army and Navy Academy, a quite impressive institution on the eastern side of Pacific Beach. I was in the second grade, was enrolled as a day student, and had the proper military uniform. Mother delivered me in the morning and collected me in the evening.

In my second grade class Lt. Massey gave a spelling test composed of words I had never seen before. Somehow I had worked on the wrong assignment. I turned to the boy behind me and asked, "Are these the right words?" Lt. Massey jumped up, pointed his finger at me, and declared, "Cheating!" I was hauled out of class and summarily sentenced to five hours in the bullpen, a small track around which I had to walk. I was to get a five minute break each hour but the upper class man assigned to supervise me wandered off. I don't know how long I had been walking, but it was hot and I was sweating. That's when Mildred showed up. She had been driving by with a client, singing the praises of the Academy, and then noticed this bedraggled boy. "My God, that's my son!" She raced over, picked me up, and that was the end of my tenure at the San Diego Army and Navy Academy.

When I was eight, I was given the freedom to go downtown by myself. Sometimes I walked, but I usually took the streetcar, which cost five cents. In those days nearly every boy my age was selling magazines, either *Liberty* or the *Saturday Evening Post*, both of which retailed for a nickel. I hit on the idea that I would sell magazines on the sidewalk in front of the Austin company. Mother gave her permission because she made sure she was in the office when I was outside. On the day the *Saturday Evening Post* was distributed, I would get on the street car after school and come to the Austin office. I am not sure how the magazines got there, but I had them to sell. Then my mother, who was not far away, took me home. That undertaking lasted about a year, and I think I made about 50 cents a week for my work.

The Austin company switched its sales efforts from Pacific Beach to Mt. Helix near La Mesa, a town considerably east of San Diego. It wasn't that all the lots in Pacific Beach had been sold, but a strange law, called the Mattoon Act, had made the property unattractive. Too, the causeway was still a government plan that had gone nowhere. The Mattoon Act was the financing vehicle for all the property improvements at Pacific Beach, with a special little twist. If one property owner did not pay his assessment, all the others were responsible for the delinquencies. As times got tough and defaults increased, it became impossible for anyone to keep his or her Pacific Beach property.

Mildred moved with the Austin company to Mt. Helix, where there was a large agricultural development. The word was avocado. The land was alleged to be the very best for cultivating this marvelous fruit, which some think of as a vegetable. I made several trips to Mt. Helix with mother and still remember the wonderful avocado ice cream. My recollection is that this Austin scheme went nowhere. Avocados were not a big hit, possibly because the economy had tanked.

That is about the last time for more than a decade when I remember my mother having anything that could be even remotely characterized as "regular income." She had committed herself to the real estate business, even though property was in the doldrums. I recall her moving among several offices and making very little at any of them. It was about 1934 when she joined C.L. Turner's office on 30th street in southern North Park, San Diego's major suburb.

In 1930, when I was 10, I won a free trip to Catalina Island for a week. Mother is seeing me off on the SS Yale.

The real estate business at that time was very different. There were no multiple listings, which have given brokers access to virtually all properties that are available in an area. In 1934 the few prospective buyers had to visit many offices because each had different properties for sale. It is surprising today, but owners had only the roughest means of setting a value on their holdings. Many were convinced to sell well under market value. The secret, of course, was to find a property that was a steal and purchase it for one's self. The price was then significantly raised, and the broker waited for a gullible person to come into the office. Only a few firms had any real volume of sales; most made ends meet by special purchases and sales.

It was a world in which Mildred did not fit. She had no money to invest and could hope only for commissions, which were virtually non-existent. Further, she was not a tough, often unscrupulous bargainer. She simply could not take advantage of people. Things were cut-throat, a world in which she did not belong. As wonderful a person as C.L. Turner was, he really knew how to play in this milieu. He had the money to invest, and he understood how to get a price down to an obscene level. Then he played the waiting game. He could not be induced to part with his gem for the market price. It had to be more. One would never think of him as a loud, boisterous salesman, but somehow he was able to convince people that what he had to sell had a special value. Things worked very well for Mr. Turner. He had a nice home and provided fully for his family. He could not be regarded as rich, but he was far better off than most in those tough times.

An exterior view of the Flower Pot. Mr. Turner's real estate sign can also be seen. The location was 33rd and El Cajon.

Mr. Turner tried in many ways to help Mildred and to get her to internalize his strategy and even to develop a hard edge. But it didn't work. And there was always the problem that she had no money to buy up the really cheap property.

With no money coming in, Mildred decided to open a flower store, the Flower Pot, next to the Turner real estate office. It was a shoe string operation, and it was really out of the active business area of North Park. My recollection is that she kept the business going there for about a year and did no better than meet her rent and expenses.

By that time the store on El Cajon blvd., where Mildred operated the Mission Fernery, was once again vacant. Since she had left, the property had been rented as a wine and beer store, as a vacuum sales and service enterprise, and as a restaurant. None prospered, and Grandma Bess had the For Rent sign on the building for some time. So it was that Mildred moved the Flower Pot back to the old digs on El

Cajon Blvd. She and Mr. Turner made a deal where he would rent about one-third of the building for his real estate office, and she took the two-thirds for her store

The question may be asked how Frank[10] made out during these very difficult economic times. The answer is very well. I don't recall ever feeling deprivation. While I knew I was not rich, it never occurred to me that I was poor. For much of my young life, I had only two priorities: a top of the line bicycle and a good tennis racket. In terms of these needs I never was in want. As I reflect on things, I have to conclude that my mother went without a lot of essentials and collaborated with my grandmother to see that I got just about everything I desired.

I do not recall, though, that I ever had an allowance. From about ages 8 to 10, my spending money came from the magazines I sold. Then I carried paper routes for two or three years, yielding at least $6 a month. Further, Grandfather Frank[8] sent money from time to time that helped out on some of the major expenditures.

When I was 13 or 14, I decided to venture into the peanut vending machine business. That involved a major investment of about $250, and I now have no idea where I got that kind of money. In any case the machines were quite lucrative. When I was 15, I was able to buy a 1928 Oakland coupe for $125, with $15 down and $10 per month. I financed that transaction out of my peanut machine earnings. Grandfather Frank[8] died in January, 1938, leaving half his estate to me. It meant that I would have $15,000-$20,000 available to me when I was 21 and could, in the meantime, draw on it for college and other personal expenses. Not much of the money was used before I went to Dartmouth, but the bequest meant I had no real money worries.

The big blow for my mother came in June, 1943, after I had finished Dartmouth and was attending the National Institute of Public Affairs in Washington. Grandma Bess died; and it is hard to describe the sense of loss we all felt. For Mildred Bess' passing was particularly traumatic because she had no one else. And Bess had been her best buddy. I might have been perceived as an anchor but my mother knew better. I was about to be drafted, and nobody knew where that would take me.

Some indication of how she felt is found in her letters, when she writes of Mr. Turner's mother and her departure for Missouri:

> You know, I am very fond of her. She is a wonderful person. It just about broke me up to talk to her, though. It seemed so good—to talk to a sweet old lady who was interested in me. There is no person quite so dear and sweet as a

beloved older person. I didn't exactly envy Mr. Turner for having his mother but I certainly wished for mine.[88]

A few months later, in September 1946, I was drafted and began my three years of service in the Army. Mother and I carried on a very active correspondence, as has been reported elsewhere. What is worth some note, however, are the boxes of goodies that she and Aunt Betty sent to me with great regularity. I believe I acknowledged every one of them in my letters home, and that meant they were reported frequently. There can be no doubt that I got the best, most treasured boxes of goodies of anyone with whom I served. Everyone knew when Frank got a new box, and they were present to share it with me. I still remember how much I prized those boxes and what they said to me about the love and support I had at home.

The Flower Pot was very modestly successful. Even during the war Mildred's income was not as much as that of a waitress or a bus driver. And much depended on a few big days like Christmas, Easter, and Valentine's Day. When I was around, I of course helped. But there times when I was back east in college. So Mother had a tremendous burden at times and got almost no sleep. Mr. Turner was always a willing helper. He was quite a sight because he knew nothing about flowers and was always neatly attired in a business suit. And he could never calculate the sales tax. Here was a man who never made a false move when his financial interests were at stake, but he did not seem to be able to figure out that the 4% sales tax on a $1 item was four cents.

One of my memories was of a visit by a woman who had been a friend of my mother and father in their Wilmington days. She appeared in 1939, and it was apparent that she was well off. She had a disdainful look on her face as she examined the circumstances of the Flower Pot, and I am sure Mother wished that none of her old friends would ever visit her. When she asked Mildred what Frank[10]'s future plans were, my mother proudly announced that I was going to Dartmouth. The woman literally snorted. "What? He won't fit in." The remark didn't bother me much, but I had the feeling it hurt Mildred greatly.

Running a small business like the Flower Pot carried many frustrations. Her letters report on many such incidents:

---

[88] *Wartime Letters from Mildred P. Sherwood to her Son Frank P. Sherwood May 29, 1944 to September 10, 1945*. Tallahassee: Florida, 2000, privately xeroxed, pgs. 5,6 (June 1, 1944)

I was closing the store when a big car rolled up. A prosperous looking couple rolled out. The man ran quick-quick to the liquor store and the woman made a wild dash into the store pushing past me at the door as if she was afraid I'd lock it before she could get in. But when she found that she would have to pay the huge sum of 60 cents for a bunch of flowers, her feathers drooped. She made for the door again, afraid I would lock her in this time, I guess.

Three weeks from this Sunday is Easter, April 1, April Fool. However, I'm not much worrying too much about it. I am going to sell plants and flowers. Gardenias, camellias, and orchids for corsages. Me—I am not going to stand up at that bench all night all alone…I'm just not in the Easter mood. I rather doubt if many people will be. For one thing there are no stockings to be had. Not unless you can get to the store early in the morning to get part of the one dozen they have to sell.

Actually, that's all that Marston's [the main department store in San Diego] puts out every day. Most of the others don't seem to have any at all. Who knows? Maybe I'll be painting stockings on my legs yet. That won't be so bad for the summer. The only trouble is Tippy [her dog] would probably lick them off. I've had one or two customers come in with their legs painted and to their utter disgust Tippy starts licking…[89]

The Pearl Harbor attack on December 7, 1941, had great significance for Mildred. Ever since she had gone into business, a Japanese flower wholesaler had been her friend and great supporter. He had extended her credit when probably no one else would have. He suffered the fate of all Japanese-Americans. He lost his business, and he and the family were shipped to an internment camp. There was no government action that disturbed Mildred more. She was one of the first to declare that Americans of Oriental descent deserved the same treatment under the law as anyone else.

While there were two different entrance doors for the Turner real estate office and the Flower Pot, there was plenty of opportunity for interaction within the building. Now mother had enough space that she could have a back room where she could do a little cooking and even relax at times. It was then that the daily lunch with Mr. Turner was institutionalized. I remember many times when I joined the two of them; and I count those sessions as some of the most enjoyable of my life. These two people had lunch together six days a week for almost ten years, with the exception of holidays when Mildred did not bother to eat.

Mildred has written in one of her letters that Mr. Turner had a very important job in the luncheon situation. He was detailed to empty the "slop bucket." While

---

[89] *Wartime Letters, op. cit.,* p. 81, March 11, 1945.

there was a sink in the back room, it was not connected to the plumbing system. (In those days everything had to be done in cast iron pipe, and so it would have been an expensive proposition.) Mother has written that one day Mr. Turner was not present for lunch, the bucket was full, and she had inadvertently allowed more water to run into it. It was a mess. She found the bucket too heavy for her to handle, and she finally got it to the back door where she dumped it outside. Her complaint was that Mr. Turner was not there when she needed him.[90] He was present in another case, reported in Mildred's letters:

> Monday I was telling Mr. Turner of my efforts to sweep up the kitchen-sitting room [the back room] Saturday. I said I wished I had some linoleum for the floor. So in the afternoon he hot-footed it out and bought a very pretty piece of linoleum. Sort of red and tan in squares. I was busy cleaning flowers when he came streaking in with it. Maybe you don't know it, but he is a very impatient guy. When he makes up his mind to do anything, it has to be then or never. So with no help he moved the furniture outdoors…[91]

Mr. Turner and Mildred

One of Mr. Turner's real admirers was my cousin, Pose. Whenever she was on one of her frequent visits, she found an occasion to get together with him, often over a drink. Pose really had to get in line because Mr. Turner had two daughters about the same age as Pose, both of whom exhibited a great fondness for their father. On one occasion Pose was in town with her two young daughters and was planning to go overnight with Mildred to Hulburd's Grove, in the San Diego back country. Pose's parents, Ross and Betty Carter, were vacationing there. When she saw Mr. Turner, Pose told him that she and Mildred would be back by 8:30 p.m.

Two sisters (Betty on left Mildred on right) are going to downtown San Diego to do some shopping and have lunch.

---

[90] *loc. cit.*
[91] *Wartime Letters, op. cit.,* p. 62

Sunday and that he should come by for a drink. Mildred wrote that she regarded the invitation as utterly ridiculous, with no expectation that Mr. Turner would appear. ("I thought, 'Is Pose ever going to get through inviting him—it's getting to be a habit' You know how good-hearted she is.") Mildred, Pose, and the kids got back about nine, and Mr. Turner was there waiting for them. He said he was worried and had been debating with himself about setting out to look for them. ("He thought maybe we had an accident and was debating what road to take to find us.")

One of the reasons for our empathy with Mr. Turner was that he was a very, very good Democrat. We had no trouble getting together on politics. Much later, in 1948, he did something that Susie [Frances] has never forgotten. He made a 14-1 bet that Harry Truman would win the presidency. Nobody believed Harry had a chance; Dewey was a shoo-in. I myself thought that a vote for Truman was wasted, and so I cast my ballot for Henry Wallace. Mr. Turner's $1,000 bet on Truman returned him $14,000. I guess we always believed that Mr. Turner was a "principled Democrat," and he got paid off handsomely.

September 1943. Mildred and her son meet for a short visit in Los Angeles before shipping out to Texas.

Grandma Bess' death changed Mildred's financial circumstances significantly. She and her sister inherited the estate equally, and my guess is that each came out with $30-40,000. It was a fairly sizeable amount and certainly gave her a security she had not known for years. On the other hand, she was back with the problem she had experienced as a young widow, namely how to secure a living from fairly limited capital.

One thing was clear. She wanted out of the Flower Pot. Mildred tried very hard to sell it, but there were no takers. Finally, in early 1946, she simply went out of business.

In our many letters, Mother and I wrote about what we would do after the war. I was completely fixed on a newspaper career, as was my dear friend, Ed Self. Mother was to be a part of the enterprise, both as an investor and as an office manager. When we did purchase the newspaper in Pacific Beach, it did not take long to discover how intense and demanding the small town newspaper is.

All the hard years in the Flower Pot had taken their toll on Mildred. Though only 51, she simply did not have the energy to become a major player in the newspaper. She much preferred to take some time off, keep house, and be a general supporter. Her investment was critical to our ability to acquire the newspaper, and so she did derive some income from the operation.

Things happened fairly rapidly. We had been settled in the house in Pacific Beach only a little more than a year when I married. We added a room to the house, and the three of us lived together. Shortly after the marriage, we sold the paper, and Frances and I were central figures in launching a fairly major publishing firm in San Diego in the North Park area. The house in Pacific Beach was sold; and Mildred bought two houses on a lot on 33rd street, just about half a block from the old Flower Pot and Mr. Turner's real estate office, which he continued to operate. Mildred lived in one house and Susie and I in the other.

The publishing firm was another one of those night and day operations. There was little time for anything, and it was Mother who often plied us with drinks and a good meal. In April, 1949, there was a major fire that effectively ended the business.

In the Fall, 1949, Frances and I moved to Los Angeles, she to complete her undergraduate studies at University of California at Los Angeles and I to begin graduate work at the University. of Southern California. Mother stayed in San Diego until late 1951. In September of that year I had been named an assistant professor at the University and was embarked on an academic career. It was clear that our future was in Los Angeles. Indeed we had built a home in Santa Monica. It was time for Mother to move north. And she did.

For about two years she worked as the receptionist at the University Press on the University of Southern California campus. It was a nice arrangement for me, and she enjoyed her work there. Things did change at the Press, however, and she chose to resign. Shortly after her arrival in Los Angeles, we began to search for a suitable place for her to live. We thought it should be near the University and should involve some rentals that would provide her income. We settled on a a large two story house, then about 50 years old, near Pico Blvd. and Hoover street. It was in an active neighborhood with a bank, food markets, drug store, cleaners, and other commercial components within a couple of blocks of the house. The location (at 1435 Arapahoe street) seemed ideal, and we had no reason to think that things would change in the foreseeable future.

The house had two apartments with the possibility of placing another one over the garage. So the heavy lifting began. We decided to convert the main house to four apartments, with a fifth over the garage. If we could pull this off, Mildred would have a reasonably good income. I had a student at the University who had built his own home and was remarkably skilled at all aspects of housing construction. He agreed to work with me. More precisely, he took on the construction job, and I was his helper. It was a very tough year, but in about 12 months we had five apartments. Mother was quite well situated. When the first apartment was listed for rent, we had an avalanche of calls. It looked like the property was a real winner.

Within a year, however, the bottom had dropped out. There was no longer a shortage of rental units in Los Angeles. Sadly, too, the Hoover-Pico area was undergoing rapid change as whites moved out and Latins and Blacks moved in. The easy rental times were over and income was inevitably down.

Mother lived in the house and managed the apartments for about six years, during which time she again tried her hand at real estate. Nothing worked very well. The real estate business was not good, and the apartments were a problem to manage. Her tenants were not the kind of people we hoped Mother would have; and it was an old house in which things went wrong.

In 1956 we bought a piece of property on which there was a small house and a second structure that was rather well built but seemed to have no function. We remodeled the house into a rather nice residence for ourselves and were able to construct quite a satisfactory one bedroom unit for mother. The situation was in many respects idyllic. We were close but there was some distance between us. Again, however, we were hit by the tremendous demographic changes in Los Angeles. When we moved to Inglewood, our area was still known as the Inglewood Poultry Colony tract, with lots of space between houses. Within a year everything had changed. The developers were beginning the process of urban "fill-in" and were building apartments on every lot they could find. About 20 units were constructed within about five feet of us. Instead of living a relatively uncluttered, almost rural life, we found ourselves in the middle of the worst kind of urban development. It did not affect Mother so much, but we knew we could not stay there as a family. By 1960 we had moved, rented our house, and Mother remained there.

In 1962 we went to Brazil, with Mother still living in Inglewood. She was now 67 and was in deteriorating health. Her teeth were false, she had high blood pressure, and she had senile diabetes.

The changes we had experienced in Inglewood had simply accentuated. Though it was an unsatisfactory step from Mildred's point of view, it seemed that the only prudent move was to sell the property to a developer to build another 20 units of apartments. Mother did not complain. We found a nice apartment for her, and she seemed relatively content.

In the summer, 1965, we went on another extended trip to Brazil and did not return until the beginning of the fall semester at the University. When Susie called Mildred to report that we were back, she got no response. She quickly went over to check on things and found Mildred collapsed on the floor. There was no telling how long she had been there. It was a disaster of the first order. Her shoulder and her arm were shattered. She was completely traumatized. I remember visiting her in the hospital and finding her essentially irrational. I had never before seen her in such a state.

After spending considerable time in recovery, we were able to bring Mildred home. I had rigged up a bell system, which would enable her to call me when she needed to go to the bathroom. Instead, she decided to go by herself. She fell; and she broke her back. She was never the same again. We tried home care but found it did not work. It was clear that she had to go to a nursing home. Nothing has been so painful to me as taking her to the nursing home and having to leave her. There is no way to feel good about warehousing older people.

After she had been in a nursing home in Inglewood more than a year, I took her by air to Charlottesville, Virginia, in July, 1968. I had accepted a position as director of the Federal Executive Institute; and happily, the nursing home was close by. The trip east was quite an experience. I had to buy two extra seats for her and then had to charter a hospital plane to carry her from Dulles Airport to Charlottesville.

Over the years she simply wasted away. It got so that she recognized only me and was completely bed-ridden. The nurse's aid would say, "Mildred, Frank is here." Mother's face would light up. But there was no communication between us. That had long been impossible.

It is perhaps consistent with all her disappointments in life that she should have spent the last eleven years as little more than a shell of a person.

APPENDIX TWO

THE "GREATEST GENERATION": BETTER TO NAME US THE "LUCKY GENERATION"

By Frank P. Sherwood

(At the outset, I want to declare that this essay does not concern those wonderful people who gave their lives or suffered severe disabilities in World War II. It is about the majority of us who served in World War II and were lucky enough to come home in one piece.)—Frank Sherwood

Introduction

World War II was the seminal event for my generation and is the way it is remembered. An editorial in the *Florida Times-Union* [December 7, 2004] on the anniversary of the Pearl Harbor attack is characteristic of the way in which my generation is described: "Those Americans who lived and fought through those times are known as the "greatest generation." Their efforts paved the way for unprecedented prosperity and secured the way of life too many of us take for granted."

The demarcation of the generations is generally murky business. Because of World War II, however, mine is more clearly defined. It consists of the males who served in that massive battle, as well as all their age cohorts, most certainly including the females. Though there are exceptions, my guess is that males who were 30 in 1941 had a likelihood of serving, thus making 1911 the first birth year of members of the generation. The same logic would suggest a male would have had to reach the age of 18 in 1945 in order to be a likely participant in the conflagration. That means people born between 1911 and 1927, a period of 16 years, are most apt to comprise my generation.

In 2006 it is therefore composed of people who range in age from 79 to 94—really old people, virtually all of them long retired. We are history. There is nothing current about my generation. It is all in the past. So why do I write this piece? Largely because the past is what I know, and I do have an interest in leaving a record of how one person saw the times and how he evaluates the claim that his generation was the "greatest."

As will become evident, I see things somewhat differently. If our greatness is simply a matter of our having overwhelmingly populated the World War II military and having been the dominant generation in a period of unprecedented economic well-being [not necessarily prosperity], then the label is correct. If greatness involves more than demographics, then I want to raise questions. Indeed, my tendency is to think of us as the "lucky generation." Serving in the military definitely cannot be considered luck, particularly for all those young people who died or were severely wounded. The luck began with Congressional actions in 1944 and continued for several decades.

Not only during the war but before it, most members of our generation did not see ourselves as overwhelmed with luck. I remember a time in college when my dear friend, Ed Self, and I were absolutely convinced that we had been born at a really miserable time. We had spent our young lives going through a disastrous depression with no real feeling that the economic conditions were ever going to improve, and now we were thrust into a war, with its possibility of premature death. We were encountering the possibility of being peremptorily killed, rather than slowly starving to death. All of this caused us to think we had in our brains the great American novel. How could a group of young people be more unfortunate? Even my mother's generation had the "roaring twenties." We had nothing we could feel good about. The idea that the "greatest generation" had it made would certainly have drawn derisive laughter. We didn't see much of a future at all.

These reflections therefore do not begin with World War II. Rather, they go back to my beginnings and the way in which I and others were shaped. While I seek to draw some generalizations about the nature of my generation, this is substantially my story and the events and circumstances I thought important to our role as key actors in an unfolding national history. Certainly the very tough times through which the nation went in the 1930's have shaped my views throughout my life. Because things turned out so much better than I would ever have expected, I feel a particular debt of gratitude to those government leaders of a previous generation who set out the policies that made all the difference for me and my generation. We did not establish the terms that have made life so good for me;

and I worry that neither we nor our successors have shown the wisdom and compassion to insure that the good times continue.

The Generation Before Us: No Great Amount of Luck

Because of the debt I feel to the previous generation and also because of an empathy for their struggles in dealing with a very difficult world, my sense of the proper departure point for this essay is my mother. She had to go through an awful lot, and the benefits I experienced never were available to her.

Because I served in World War II and am 25 years younger than my mother, we are presumed to be members of different generations. Yet she and I shared the experiences of the Great Depression and of the War. I exclude my father because he died at age 34, at a time when his career was just under way. Had he lived, there is no doubt that the experience of my mother and me would have been very different. He was an established professional [when there were relatively few in the society], had already begun to accumulate assets, and would undoubtedly have negotiated the great difficulties of the Depression far better than we did.

My mother was born in 1895, married in 1918, and delivered her only child in 1920, when she was 25. By the time of her marriage, she was a registered nurse and was head of an infirmary. After his death, she had nothing more to do with the nursing profession because of the trauma she experienced in caring for him as he suffered a painful cancer death. She returned to her parents' home in San Diego with some money and no idea what she would do. The twenties were identified as boom times, but the support system was very different from what we know today. There were no schools she could attend that would enable an intelligent, fairly well-educated person to identify new career options. Furthermore, she was a woman. Sex limited her options greatly. [She did not consider marriage because her man was dead.] She ended up in real estate and did modestly well in 1927-30, selling subdivision lots. When the Depression struck, the bottom fell out of all such ventures [and about everything else], and my mother was out of a job.

She stayed in real estate and made very little in the ensuing years. She knew the business, was smart, helpful, and a person with whom you would like to do business. Why did things go so badly for her? First, there was essentially no business, with very little income to be shared. Depending on commissions from sales, as she did, meant little money because there few sales, with essentially no financing available. There were no multiple listings, which has made it possible to tap into the total inventory of housing in a community today. Then, if you found a house someone wanted to sell at a bargain price [essentially everything was for sale], you kept it for yourself. So it was tough to develop and market a group of really saleable houses. The few who made it in the real estate business had some capital and were engaged in trading their own properties. My impression is that it helped in those days to be cunning, somewhat devious, and at times dishonest. These were traits that my mother simply did not have. If she had been active in the latter part of the 20th century, with much more accessible financing, multiple listings, and a more mobile society, I think she would have done very well. I have had enough dealings with real estate people to know that those who are smart, informed, responsible, honest, and industrious do quite well. But that was not the way things were in the 30's.

My mother eventually opened a small flower shop and remained in that business until the end of World War II. At the store's height during the war, she employed two people and made a wage, working 12 hours a day, six days a week. But it was only a wage. She tried to sell the business after the war. Nobody wanted it. She inherited some money from my Grandmother and that became her nest egg for the future.

In 1945, she was 50. A woman of that age was generally regarded as grandmotherly. There were few places in the work society for her. Further, it was unreasonable to expect such an individual could develop assets that would comfortably carry her into old age. One of the great social programs of the 20th century, Social Security, was established in 1935, and my mother achieved eligibility in 1960. Her pension was the minimum, about $30 per month. But do not make light of it. That was a major piece of her income.

My mother was an able, intelligent, and industrious person, equipped in many ways to contribute to the society. It says something about the times and the circumstances that she was never given a real opportunity to do so. Had she been born later, I am sure she would have been fully as great a contributor to the society as anyone in my generation. Those who came later, were fortunate to live in times when there was recognition that governments could do a lot to make life better for people.

The Depression was a Disaster for Everyone Living at the Time

The difficulties my mother was experiencing dominated my life in many ways. It was not just my mother's situation that created a major impact. Economic tragedy engulfed me. I remember going downtown with my mother and her observing to me that all the banks were closed. I don't think there is anything more detrimental to human dignity than being told there is no place for you in the society. That is what the massive unemployment of the time did, leaving people with no means to contribute usefully to the society. The experience of the 30's produced profound, continuing effects on the way in which I saw the world. I have never quite believed, for example, in the stability and continuing vitality of the business world. I saw it when it was essentially on its back.

Fortunately, I was more an onlooker than a participant. I always had adequate shelter and good food, largely because of my grandmother. She had a number of real estate investments that produced enough income, even in those tough times, to keep the family afloat.

I recognized the catastrophic difficulties of the times most fully when I worked as a classified advertising salesman for the San Diego Sun, the third daily newspaper in the town, in 1938. Read most accounts of the Depression, and you learn the Depression was over by 1938. It was not. I covered car dealers, furniture stores, and real estate firms. None of them were doing much business; and, indeed, many were on the edge of bankruptcy. Rents on buildings were far in arrears; yet owners hesitated to move people out because they knew their stores would simply sit empty. There were houses for rent all over the town; but the ads for them in our paper did not pull. Nobody answered them. The other two newspapers in town, both owned by the same company, had larger circulations and were more powerful. But we had more than 20,000 subscribers. You'd think there would be at least some response to advertisements in our paper. There weren't.

I worked six days a week, eight hours a day, with no allowance for the necessary use of my car, and was paid $12 per week. That's right, 25 cents an hour. But I doubt I really earned my pay. Demoralization was everywhere. I don't remember a day when I sold a lot of advertising.

Later, I became editor of a small weekly newspaper. It was the same story, except that the pay was even less, $5 a week. I never complained because I don't think the publisher was taking in much more than that.

It was during that time I set a target for my future earnings peak: $50 per week. That was the salary of the local advertising manager of *The Sun*, a high level position in the organization. That was also the top of the pay scale for high school teachers, a reasonable possibility for me. If I had been asked at the time, "Would you settle for that, right now?", my answer would certainly have been yes. I remember my boss, *The Sun* classified advertising manager, very well. He was an older man, extremely intelligent, a graduate of Grinnell College, and an alcoholic. He dropped dead of a heart attack before I left the paper. I don't imagine his salary could have been more than $35 a week. Heaven knows what kinds of disappointments he experienced as a member of my mother's generation.

I stayed out of school for a year and a half before going on to the college. As I reflect on the reasons, it was basically because I had severe anxieties about my capacity to make a reasonable living. I was not at all sure college would help me cope with that terrific problem. I figured I ought to get out in the real world and determine how tough the going was. As I found out, it was very, very tough. I think I went back to college partly because I wanted to postpone the evil day when things were really on the line.

My Life Changes: Enter World War II and the Early Post-War Years

The anxieties about our future developed even before Pearl Harbor. It was in early 1940, when I was still in my Freshman year, that the Nazis unleashed their *blitzkrieg* on the unprepared nations of Europe. The fall of the Maginot Line in France and the disastrous British retreat from Dunkirk were particularly unsettling. I was taking a Political Science class with a man who had been an infantry captain in World War I, and so he was regarded as a great expert. We spent much of the class time discussing the disasters the Allies were experiencing and left each session thoroughly deflated. I think we all knew the involvement of the U.S. was not long off.

I walked into the Dartmouth Library Sunday night, December 7, and there was a little sign on the check-out desk, "The Japanese have bombed Pearl Harbor." Minutes later, it seemed, the whole campus was buzzing. Now we knew our lives were soon to change radically. This was not going to be a war where a few would be involved. We knew we would all be in it, and I am sure none of us wanted it any other way. Ed Self, and I were most assuredly not hawks. We had been in a high school where we learned the truth about World War I and what a tragedy it was for everyone. Yet, depressed as we were, we believed absolutely that we had to defend our country. After all, our enemies were the aggressors. The difference in feeling about our World War II and those that came later, Viet Nam and Iraq in particular, was huge. We really believed that the homeland was threatened and that we were the defenders.

During the War, I wrote many letters to my mother, all of which she saved. [They are now collected in a single volume, which members of my family and some libraries have.] In a number of them, particularly ones written from Europe when I was an officer, I speculated on my future. By that time I held a college degree, with some graduate work and, was an "officer and a gentleman." Yet I saw little promise in the future. I wrote that my expectations were modest, that I would likely struggle to make a living, and that it would be important to observe severe constraints on material needs. In effect, I resigned myself to a lower middle class life. In one respect, however, I had outlandish ambitions. I really did hope that Ed Self and I could get together in the newspaper business and have a major publishing success. Some of that came true, but I never really trusted the business world. The thirties had left an indelible impression on me. In business you might be on top one day and busted the next. That was why I did not dare to hope that I would ever enjoy anything but a modest living.

Very few of us probably had any big aspirations for the future. We wanted to get home, pick up with our families, and be free of the War. That was enough. The struggles of the 30s no longer looked so bad.

The major event assuring me that things were not going to be so dismal in the future was my appointment to the faculty of the University of Southern California as an assistant professor in the fall, 1951, almost exactly five years after I had been demobilized. What made that such a significant watershed was that I now had a job I could regard as permanent. I would no longer be subject to the quixotic turbulence of the marketplace. It is true that universities are in many respects "ivory towers." Their isolation from economic ups and downs was a great solace to me. I started service in the University at a nine-month salary of $4000, which some thought low. From my point of view, however, it was plenty good. Susie and I lived well on it. In point of fact, I made considerably more than that through other assorted assignments. For a person who developed his basic coding in the 30s, things have worked out wondrously well.

How to account for so much good luck? Do I, as a member of the "greatest generation", deserve credit for having fashioned my own destiny? I think not.

What Really Won World War II

And that brings me to a more analytical, less autobiographical, view of how we can account for the good times that people of my generation enjoyed.

The quotation from the *Florida Times-Union* is relevant because it epitomizes what the popular culture has concluded from the Tom Brokaw book on the "greatest generation", namely that we young soldiers won the war and fashioned the prosperity that followed.

There can be no dispute about two things. The U.S., with its allies, were clearly the victors. Those of us who saw the destroyed Germany in 1945 can attest to how complete that triumph was. Second, there was a special group of people who experienced combat and exercised the brute force that resulted in our conquest. Just because a person wore a uniform, however, did not mean that he risked his life and engaged in the raw struggles involved. When I was in Europe, I often heard that four out of five soldiers there were not in combat roles. They were important, of course, to the prosecution of the effort but they were no more likely to encounter the enemy than someone at a war plant in the U.S. As a member of the G-3 staff in the forward command post of the 99th Army Division, I was assumed to be in combat and therefore was awarded two battle stars. But I never had a face-to-face encounter with a German. My life was never at risk.

It has always offended me that we do not seem to make a distinction between those who made the assault on Normandy and those who were engaged in backup roles in England. The reality is that few of the "greatest generation" were in combat and can even make a pretense that they were war heroes. We should reserve our plaudits for a relatively small percentage of the 16 million men and relatively few women who served in the U.S. armed forces. Those who were in combat deserve our undying gratitude. They were really special. And we must be particularly mindful of those who sacrificed their lives for what they undoubtedly considered a noble cause. The rest of us made sacrifices in terms of time lost for an essentially destructive purpose, worked plenty hard, and didn't make much money. But we weren't spectacular in any way. We filled niches and made contributions that were not much different from those of people on the home front. Once you exclude those who really did the fighting from the rest of us, it seems to me the "greatest generation" blends in with Americans of all generations who were doing what they could to end things successfully.

A Highly Segregated Military

There was one aspect of the military in World War II that does not project a picture of unity and camaraderie. Our Army [and I believe the other branches as well] was a totally segregated operation. When I reported for the draft in September 1943, in San Diego, I found myself associating especially with a very pleasant, affable black man. We sat together on the train to San Pedro; but, once having arrived at Fort McArthur, we were separated and I never saw him again. I assume he went some place to learn how to drive a truck. In my three years in the Army, I don't remember having any real contact with a black person. No black even served in the mess hall, if my memory serves me correctly. Texas was typical of the old South in my days of basic training—separate drinking fountains, restrooms, waiting rooms, restaurants, and everything else. You certainly got no feeling that we were "in this together."

There was no riskier job in the world than the infantry. The blacks were excluded from even that kind of service until very late in the war.

I was assigned to the anti-tank platoon of an infantry company in basic training; became a linesman for an infantry company in the 10th Mountain Division, and received my commission at Fort Benning, Georgia as a 2nd Lieutenant of Infantry. We all recognized that we platoon leaders, along with the men who served with us, had a short life expectancy. That is the way modern wars are. Yet the society did not permit blacks even an opportunity to volunteer for such service. It is amazing that not a single black was being prepared at Fort Benning to serve in the most expendable role in the Army, 2nd Lieutenant of Infantry.

Toward the end of the war, shortages of cannon fodder for the front line began to appear, and so more interest developed in assigning blacks to such duty.

According to a book on using blacks in the infantry in my division, the 99th, many blacks volunteered and wanted to serve in combat roles. At the tail end of the war, several extra infantry units of blacks were added to the 99th and acquitted themselves well. What shocks me now was that I was in G-3, the operations staff arm of the division, and I never knew that we had black components in our organization. It was obviously very hush-hush, which shows just how sensitive the idea of integration was.

The separation of the races probably led to more bigotry than would have occurred with easier and more frequent interaction. White officers often found themselves commanding black units. It was constantly reported to us how unruly the blacks were. The blacks were not even allowed to have one of their own provide leadership in a motor pool. And I found myself sharing the prejudice. I remember the thing that I feared most, when we traveled to Europe on the old luxury liner, Aquitania, was that I would be put in command of a contingent of blacks. I wasn't given such a responsibility, for which I was always grateful. Even when I was leaving Germany and was in Bremerhaven for a couple of weeks in 1946, I had the same fear that I would be put in charge of black troops. Again, it did not happen. I do not recall there being any blacks on the victory ship which transported me back to the U.S. Very likely, they went on their own ship, with a few white officers telling them what to do.

The Impersonal Army—Like the Factories Back Home

A problem of a different sort emerged from the approach General George C. Marshall took to organizing and managing the Army. When I was serving, I felt the Army was a huge, impersonal place and did not understand why. Many years later, I read the book by Stephen Ambrose, *Citizen Soldier,* and then understood the source of my feeling. As Marshall conceptualized it, most of the Army, i.e. combat soldiers, were interchangeable and replaceable. When a soldier was killed, injured, or otherwise withdrawn from duty, the idea was to have another person available, trained, and ready to move into his position. Since there was a constant parade of casualties, the infantry division was very much like an assembly line, with new, identical parts constantly being pulled from the replacement bin and put into action. The bin from which people were drawn was the replacement depot, popularly known as the "repple depple." We arrived at the depot from numerous points of origination, trained together in some degree for two weeks to a month, and then went our separate ways as replacements to a great variety of units. We typically never saw each other again. As Ambrose described it, the result was a society of strangers. It was particularly tough in combat, Ambrose reported, where so much depended on mutual trust. The old timers were not at all confident about the newcomers, and the newcomers were not sure there was anyone they could trust. I did not have combat experience, but I do recall the feeling of *anomie* I had in the replacement depot. I perceived myself very much alone in that vast sea of people.

Not all the Army was like that, but most of it got that way. For a long time, the 10th Mountain was a family of 10,000 people who had been together for a couple of years. Then, shortly after its shipment to Texas, the decision was made that the 10th would be a regular division, and 4,000 flatland soldiers were added to its ranks. Ultimately, this large influx of non-skiers was assimilated into the culture; and the 10th's performance in Italy showed that the old family feeling was still present. But the Army had done about all it could to destroy the bonds of the organization. I have a friend who served as a commander of an artillery battery, which began in North Africa, moved into Sicily, and then into Southern France. As artillery, they did not suffer the heavy casualties and fairly much stayed together for four years. The members of the battery consider themselves old comrades, and they continue to have close relations. I never experienced anything like that, and I think I am more typical.

The Germans were more apt to follow the family approach. Even units that suffered heavy casualties retained their organizational integrity and fought on with very much diminished numbers. The 99th Division G-2 did not just provide us with an order of battle but supplied detailed estimates on the size of the units we were facing. It was frequently the case that German divisions were at less than half their authorized strength. That is in contrast to one of our most famous U.S. divisions, the 1st, whose numbers of soldiers serving during the War years amounted to about four times its authorized strength. Only the commanders and staff people were stable elements in the organization.

Since we won the war, one has to assume that our industrial model for the Army worked best. However, the Germans, with their family model, put up one hell of a fight. I was involved in combat only in January-April, 1945, when it was no longer a question who was going to win but when. I think we were all impressed with how courageously the Germans fought with very little left of their former military might. Their infantry divisions were just ghosts of their former selves. Once in awhile we would see a lone enemy plane in the sky, not able to do any damage; and the much feared 88s, a truly lethal artillery weapon, were so few as to be only a nuisance.

The Real Secret of Our Success: Unbelievable Production

The pitiful state of the German military came home to me dramatically when we crossed the Remagen bridge on the Rhine River (the first full division to do so) and found ourselves taking over a major German field hospital. It was in sad condition; and my greatest shock was that the bandages used in this significant facility were made of paper.

When you get right down to it, what made the U.S. military so dominant world wide was the awesome manufacturing capacity that had appeared almost overnight in North America. What we produced in a few short years—in weaponry, ships, airplanes, vehicular transportation—was simply phenomenal. This was particularly so given the almost lifeless industrial plant of the 30s. Suddenly we produced the ships to overwhelm the Japanese in the Pacific, created the shipping capacity to deliver scads of goods all over the world, and manufactured so many airplanes that we rather quickly dominated the skies. All this while we were still producing an unbelievable amount of food.

I certainly saw the consequences of this production marvel in Europe. There was, of course, the air supremacy we secured. We drove the Messerschmidts from the skies. In my relatively few days in combat, we never worried about enemy air attacks. What was really impressive was the way in which our bombers flattened whole cities. I never saw Dresden, which was apparently wiped out in a night; but I witnessed Frankfurt, Nuremberg, and Wurzburg, where hardly a single building was standing. The devastation was astounding and virtually all of it imposed on civilians. At the time I can't say I was sad about all this. Good enough for the Krauts, I thought.

Later, when I was in Military Government, I really wondered. There were two incidents that particularly struck me. One was told to me by a woman, half-Jewish, who had no reason to love the Nazis. She was in Wurzburg when the American bombers hit and destroyed one-third of the town in a single night. She described the trauma that all the residents—women, children, and older people—experienced as they rushed to the fields to escape the explosions and then the fires that engulfed the historic city. Later, the bombers came back and finished the demolition of Wurzburg. The other case involved a man, about 50, who was in charge of our officers' mess in Bamburg, about 30 miles north of Nuremberg. He was a pleasant fellow, and we had a good relationship. So it was not surprising that he asked to hitch a jeep ride with me to Nuremberg. When we got into the city, which was nothing but ruins, he asked that we detour a couple of blocks from the street we were traveling. Suddenly he asked the driver to stop. We were in front of nothing but a pile of rocks. "There is my life," he said. The rubble was all that was left of the once-flourishing restaurant he had spent most of a lifetime building.

An unforgettable demonstration of American military might was afforded me as the 99th stopped on the west side of the Rhine River. We were to allow an armored division to pass through our lines. I had never seen a full division, let alone an armored one, before. The parade of this mechanized division went on for more than 12 hours. It was a spectacle I shall never forget. I developed a full appreciation of why we had become invincible.

Thus I quarrel with the assertion that the "greatest generation" won the war. We handled the equipment that made the difference, and perhaps we deserve some credit for not screwing things up. But it was all the generations working together, and making their own sacrifices, that really provided the wherewithal for our great victories. In 1943, when I went in the Army, my father would have been 55, certainly at the peak of his powers as a professional chemist. Further, he had the experience that would have been invaluable in World War II. He had been a chief technologist at a major war plant in World War I. It would have been people like my father providing the leadership, the experience, and the knowledge to guide the manufacturing miracle on the home front in 1940-45.

Yet his generation does not even have a name. If you accept the conclusions of the Brokaw book, he was largely irrelevant. Brokaw fastened on the truly inspirational cases of a few people to tell a compelling story about a part of World War II. It probably never occurred to him that the naming of his book would end up as perhaps the most popular—and altogether wrong—generalization about the people involved in World War II.

My Generation Was in the Right Place After the War—Luck?

I now come to the second assertion in the *Times-Union*, namely that the "greatest generation"…"paved the way" for the good economic times that followed. Things were a great deal more complicated.

Inheritors of an Industrial Might Dating Back to Alexander Hamilton

In the first place, you simply did not shut down the immense economic capacity that magically appeared in the war years. That huge strength undoubtedly went back to World War I, where it was the U.S. goods, not so much soldiers, that defeated the Germans. This brawn was undoubtedly there during the 30s but largely latent, to be exploited anew in the 40s. Thus the mighty power of the United States came from the contributions of many generations, perhaps dating back to Alexander Hamilton.

After the war, we had essentially no economic competition. We were the only kids on the block. The rest of the developed world was devastated, culturally as well as economically. It's hard to believe now that a pack of cigarettes would buy you a bottle of fairly good champagne in the Paris of 1946. All we had to do was follow our fathers and keep on producing. Anything American was an easy sell—

and at a good price. And our currency was the strongest and most prized in the world. As late as 1962, by which time some of the European countries had begun to get back on their feet, the Chevrolet was the most desired car in Brazil, where I was then working. It could be sold for far more than its original price. The reason was that the Chevrolet was considered to be the very best car in the world, largely because it was American.

I used to say that the "American Century" lasted about 20 years, from 1945 to 1965. By 1965, both the Germans and the Japanese were getting back on their feet and producing high quality items. We could no longer assume we were the best. We had to face the fact that we lived in a competitive world. For the next two decades we did not do so well. It was in the 90s, when the "baby boomers" began to take charge, that we once again found areas in which we could dominate economically.

My sense is that the "greatest generation" was a so-so performer from the economic standpoint. Things had to go well in the 1945-65 period because we had no competition; but we had plenty of rough times in the more than two decades that followed. In many ways our parents got things started and our kids picked up the slack in the 90s. My generation is certainly out of the game today, and we will see who we want to blame for our mediocre economic performance since 2000.

It is true, of course, that there have been immense advantages to living in the last half of the 20th century. What I have called the luck of my generation may be incorrectly characterized. We were the beneficiaries of significantly helpful government policies and programs. A weak, do-nothing government, which seems to be the preference today, would not have produced the conditions which made life secure and profoundly satisfying over the last half century. I take no credit for these gains, nor do I think my generation should.

Major Governmental Programs that Made the Difference and Caused Us to Look Good

There were several major government programs that have made the big difference: the GI Bill, Social Security, a number of pieces of housing legislation, and Medicare. Only Medicare can be said to be a product of our generation.

The GI Bill of Rights and Its Educational Benefits

By far the most important of these government programs for me was the GI Bill of Rights, originally known as the Serviceman's Readjustment Act, passed when Franklin Delano Roosevelt was still alive, in 1944. It contained education and housing provisions that had profound societal consequences.

Most people may not recognize the importance of the GI Bill because it affected only about 10% of the population, all of them members of the "greatest generation." What FDR's government did was provide an opportunity for all those who had been in the armed services, regardless of rank, sex or color, to get more education. Imagine its significance. We were saying to the great majority of young men [and a few women] in America, some 16 million of them, "Go back to school and the government will pay." Nothing like that had ever happened before. It is one of the great philanthropies of all time, and it produced tremendous dividends. All the young men who left college, such as my friends at Dartmouth, and patriotically volunteered for military service, were now encouraged to go back and complete their education at government expense. A friend recounts this experience. He found himself demobilized in 1945, a young man at sea with a wife and no skills. It was a GI counselor and a GI program that rescued him. He was hired by a business as an apprentice, the point at which he should have entered five years earlier. While the business paid him only an apprentice's wages, the government added a supplement in recognition of the fact that my friend had spent five years in the Air Force, a period when he would normally have been improving his skills and thus his earning capacity in civilian life. Later, my friend, who had never given a thought to going to college, left the firm and used his GI bill to get his bachelor's degree. He served for many years as a high school teacher.

This story is a very common one. The most exciting thing about the education provision of the GI bill was that it enabled people to realize their hopes and aspirations. They could be all they wanted to be. I became fully aware how immense was the consequence of the GI bill when I served on the faculty of the Federal Executive Institute, then the senior staff college of the Federal government. We had small group meetings where we explored the backgrounds of senior executives, who were on average 45 years old, and helped them identify new goals for the remainder of their public service. One story was regularly repeated. It was of a farm boy who entered the military with little more thought of the future than to return to the farm. When he got out, he found he had a chance to go to college at government expense. In almost every case this boy was the first in his family to earn a degree. Such individuals obviously did not return to the farm; and some of them rose to positions of great responsibility in the Federal government. It has always been my conviction that they contributed tremendously to the quality of our government. Others, of course, moved into professions that would otherwise have been foreclosed to them—medicine, law, architecture, higher education, and so forth. The GI Bill provided our society with quality human resources that would have not otherwise been available. And that had enormous economic consequence.

While the GI bill allowed people to move into the most elevated of professions, it also did wonders to improve capacity to perform in less exalted roles. In my earliest days as a professor at the University of Southern California in the 50s, I found myself teaching classes composed entirely of Los Angeles City police officers. Most were going for a two-year certificate, and many proceeded from there to a bachelor's degree. A few even earned advanced degrees. They were all supported by the GI bill. This was a talented group of people, though I had trouble with some of their political/social convictions. They were the reason the Los Angeles Police Department was then regarded as the best in the country. The cream flowed to the top, and a few of my students became the chiefs not only in LA but across the country. It is one small example of the way in which the GI bill affected all aspects of our lives.

In my own case I used the GI bill to secure my PhD at the University of Southern California. I had been in the publishing business for three years after the war and had my successes and setbacks. The bottom line is that I did not like business. It was too unpredictable, too demanding, and too frenetic. I wanted to do something that provided at least a little leisure and demanded more use of the mind. In 1949 I had no idea where those types of expectations would lead me. Certainly I did not anticipate that I would end up with a career of nearly 45 years in higher education. One of the beauties of the GI bill is that I did not have to tell anyone what my educational objectives were. It was enough to enroll. In point of fact, my reason for entering the PhD program was not a very compelling one. I wanted to buy a little time, with the excuse to myself that I was pursuing the PhD because my father had one.

The GI bill was not generous but it was adequate. I got a part-time job at the University Press; and that, with the GI stipend, allowed a modest living. Susie finished her degree at UCLA and then got a job. When that occurred, we were in clover and moved to a nice apartment on the beach in Santa Monica.

It turned out that I was an exceptionally good student and attracted faculty attention. My reputation, plus a desperate need for more professors in the School of Public Administration, led to a job offer. That employment opportunity, incidentally, was another consequence of the GI Bill, which had caused enrollment in the School to surge and thus created the need for more faculty. The School did something it had never done before: hired one of its own. In 1951 I was made an assistant professor on the tenure track. In 1954 I was promoted to associate professor and given tenure; in 1957 I was appointed a full professor. It was a spectacular career progression. While I can take some credit for what happened, the real truth is that I was in the right place at the right time. And I was there because of the GI bill.

I have often wondered how things would have turned out in a GI bill-less world. I am sure I would not have sought a PhD, partly because I had no idea what I would do with it and also because the only way we could have handled it was for Susie to get a job and support me. That would not have appealed to me. Destiny works in strange ways, and perhaps I would have experienced some other lucky breaks along life's way. It is hard to believe, however, that my life would have been as varied and challenging as it turned out to be. The likelihood, I think, is that I would have gotten a job in the San Diego school system as a teacher and stayed there until retirement. It is clear that the GI Bill dramatically changed my life.

Overall, I see the educational benefits of the GI Bill as having contributed immensely to the economic development of the United States. We greatly increased the quality of our work force through that massive investment in education. Nothing like it has occurred before or since. Further, its consequences continued long after my generation had exhausted its education benefits. It changed the aspirations of the society. It is now an assumption that a successful career starts with a college education. And these aspirations have been met with a dramatic expansion of the higher education plant, largely in the public sector. It is now possible for the great majority of our young people to find a way to attend college. Our private institutions have not suffered because many of the "baby boomers" have had their own version of the GI Bill, financed by their parents who appreciate the value of education.

A Second Great Piece of the GI Bill: Advancing Home Ownership and Making the House an Economic Asset

As I reported above, the GI Bill contained another highly significant feature, help for GIs to own their own homes. Since nearly 70 per cent of the population now possesses the deed to their houses, we may think things have always been that way. That certainly is not the case. The dramatic increase in home ownership since World War II inevitably embraced my generation. We were the willing recipients of aid from our government, with significant long-term effects. Data make it clear that the house is the most significant economic asset of most Americans, and so programs that made this possible must be given great credit for our prosperity/affluence in the last half of the 20th century.

Real estate has been a very good investment during this period and has accounted for a great share of societal wealth. That's understandable because this has been a period of extreme population growth. As more people pour into the country and covet their own chunk of land, they put pressure on prices. And, as we might expect, the pressure is greatest where the new arrivals are most numerous. There is no generational dimension to all this. My generation did not shrink the land to make it more valuable. We might have had something to do with levels of immigration but that was largely through inaction. We did very little to stop people from coming.

It is also obvious that some land is more valuable that others. South Dakota does not have the same attraction as San Diego. So various pieces of land appreciate spectacularly because they are so desirable. A friend owns a lot on the Gulf of Mexico in the Florida Panhandle. Back when I was first aware of the property nearly 20 years ago it had a worth of $25,000. In 2004 the minimum price was $600,000—a 2400 per cent increase. That is not unusual. That is common. My friend did not do anything to enhance its value. He simply had the good sense to keep the land on the beach.

In other cases land values have been greatly enhanced by government actions—orders on land use, roads and highways, and utilities. The land itself has not changed, but the value assigned to it has—dramatically. These are all examples of what Henry George called "unearned increments." Owners have done nothing intrinsically to improve the land and yet it has become infinitely more valuable. Immense wealth has been created. Certainly my generation has benefitted from this kind of development, but largely as relatively passive participants.

While gains from real estate transactions have probably provided increased wealth to a relatively small segment of the population, housing is different. Many have seen major gains in their economic assets, simply by staying in the same place. Once, housing was largely seen in terms of its significance in sustaining life. While that is still the case [and it is good that so many people—but not all—have quite adequate shelter], the house as a highly negotiable financial asset constitutes a big change. It has contributed greatly to our sense of prosperity/affluence in the last half of the 20th century.

There is so much that made home ownership accessible to an increasing number of Americans over the last 75 years that it is hard for most people to conceive of anything different. Before 1935, however, possessing your own shelter was not easy. Though I was young, I became well aware of the problems involved. The home in which I grew up was purchased by my grandparents in 1905 for $5000. They made a down payment of $3000 and got a mortgage of $2000. But that mortgage was nothing like the ones we know today. First, it was for only five years and second, it had no amortization feature. You paid the interest; and, at the end of five years, you still owed $2000. You then had to get a new mortgage, and you hoped the economy was in good enough shape to make that possible. Thirty years after the initial purchase, my grandmother was still paying interest on a $2000 mortgage. I remember the great anxiety as to whether she would be able to find new mortgage money. Luckily, she did. Today, of course, things would be very different. That mortgage would long since have been paid off.

My mother's experience with mortgages was somewhat similar but more unfortunate. She had bought two houses, one a duplex, with my father's insurance money. She made a big down payment and financed the small amount still owed. The mortgages, which may have been for only three years, came due and she could not get new ones. She lost the properties. If she had been paying off the principal over a longer period of time, that would never have happened. She would have continued to own the properties.

In effect, the extent of housing ownership in a society depends on four factors: the size of the down payment required; the availability of mortgage money, the rate of mortgage interest charged; and the terms and conditions for paying off the mortgage. In the cases with which I was familiar as a boy, the mortgage itself was the most troublesome.

Early in the New Deal, these kinds of problems were addressed. Clearly, Franklin Roosevelt wanted to make home ownership more available for a greater number of Americans. Not only were efforts made to reduce the down payments and also lower interest payments, largely by the government's guaranteeing mortgages, but also the idea of loan amortization was adopted. It was so sensible that amortization quickly became the norm for public and private loans. Amortization meant that owners paid interest and a small share of the principal owed on a monthly basis. The Home Owners' Loan Corporation [HOLC] was only one of a number of agencies that made the terms easier for people to buy homes. The problems my mother and grandmother encountered were largely eliminated through amortization.

It was within this context that the GI Bill of Rights was framed in 1944 to help veterans with their shelter needs after the war. Through loan guarantees, the GI Bill made down payments and interest rates the lowest they had ever been. In the 1950s, you automatically knew that a GI-financed house was going to be the most affordable you could find. Much of this housing was in subdivisions, incidentally, and the government used its leverage to keep housing prices in line. I, like most other veterans, used the GI bill to buy a house. It was very good value, and the terms were affordable. I sold the house later, made a profit on it, and thus added to my financial assets. I followed a pattern that became standard at the time of selling and using the profit to buy a somewhat better house. For my generation the move upward was slow, but it was nevertheless consistent. The GI Bill fostered financing arrangements that permitted virtually all GIs to realize their aspirations of owning their own homes.

This trend simply became more pronounced as time went on. New institutions were introduced, both in the public and private sectors, that further facilitated home buying. The semi-public organizations, such as GNMA, Freddie Mac, and Fannie Mae, which purchase individual mortgages, pool them, and then sell shares to the investing public, handled a problem which had been persistent, the ebb and flow of mortgage money. When I tried to get my last mortgage in 1983, I had a real difficulty. It was a time when there was no mortgage money; and so I had to pay 13% interest. Today that is no longer a problem. There is a constant turnover of mortgages, and the redemption money is continually recycled.

There is no doubt that my generation, as have succeeding ones, benefitted from all such housing reforms. Increasing housing values have simply made things better. A friend my age has stayed in his house for 40 years and has seen its value ratchet up from about $30,000 to about $700,000. The house I bought in 1983 for $100,000 was sold in 2001 for $240,000. My son's first house in Washington DC, which he bought less than 20 years ago, cost him about $35,000 and the one he now owns is valued at about $3,500,000. Of course, he has a substantial mortgage and has made investments in his properties [this is his third house in that time], but there is no doubt this house is a very major financial asset.

There is no doubt that my generation has prospered greatly. Indeed, there is the frequent report that we have, are, and will be providing our children with the largest inheritances in American history. The question, of course, is how much of this has been our doing and how much is simply being in the right place at the right time. Personally, I think those who deserve the credit are the executive and legislative leaders in the Roosevelt years, and particularly those who were involved in the GI Bill of Rights. They were certainly not of our generation and most likely were of my mother's.

Retirement with Independence, Dignity and Security: More Luck?

What has been written about the "greatest generation" has been confined to that small space of time when World War II consumed us all, rather than the long slog afterwards when we progressed through the bulk of our lives. We typically left the work scene at age 65, when a new phase of our lives generally began.

Since most people in past generations have died not long after their active years, retirement is a relatively new concept. It also has become more significant with urbanization. My great grandfather ran his large farm until the day he died, at age 95. In the days when farming was the main occupation in the U.S., the old man was in charge until he lost his mental and physical capacities, supported increasingly in the work on the farm by his children. I suspect there was no sharp transition between work and non-work. Further, housing was probably not a great issue. Structures were owned by families for generations and simply passed on as time demanded.

That was not the case in urban communities. In these places there developed a sharp distinction between work and non-work. You had a job, worked at it for years, and it was suddenly decreed that you were too old for the task. The move to retirement often meant a person had lost a sense of value and purpose. Even more sadly, the basic means of support had disappeared. Cities also had very little of the stability of the farms. People moved around incessantly. Family structures were weakened because the kids had moved away. The idea of everyone living together became unrealistic, leaving old people with inadequate shelter and food. [Medicine became a problem later.] When I was a boy, talk about older people led to talk about poverty.

We are the "lucky generation" because we are the first who are not old and impoverished. Since the fates treated us kindly and we may be the wealthiest generation, still there were relatively few who could set aside enough money fully to sustain them in old age. Social Security has been the great mainstay. Over half the people on Social Security today depend on it for at least two-thirds of their income and 20% have only Social Security to sustain them.

I think of these issues in terms of my mother. As I have mentioned, she received a Social Security stipend of about $30 for the last few years of her ambulatory and active life. If she had remained healthy, there is not much doubt she would have ended up living with us. My income was insufficient to allow me to set her up in a separate household. So, from my perspective, the problem of the old and poor was right at the doorstep of my generation.

What caused the momentous change for us? New retirement approaches and policies that began to appear in the 1920s and were greatly expanded in the 1930s. It takes a long time for these kinds of societal reforms to build up a head of steam. My mother's very small Social Security stipend in 1960-65 is indicative of that. It was my generation that realized the full benefit of these programs. Again, luck.

Social Security Created in 1935: The Base for our Retirement Systems Today

Clearly, the big step forward in achieving pensions for the retired elderly was the Social Security Act of 1935. This was a major part of FDR's New Deal Program, and so he, among other enlightened members of Congress, must be given credit for securing this monumental change in our social system. It was a reform already achieved in many European countries; and we simply adopted the enlightened social policies of others. Nevertheless, it was a hugely significant move that was to have its consequences for decades. Social Security made retirement an idea "in good currency." While I think of Social Security in terms of retirement, it is important to remember that it also covers those who are permanently disabled and the children of those who died prematurely. As with the GI Bill, our national policy leaders were generous and progressive in conceiving how the national government should support and serve its people. If it were not for their willingness to put larger social interests above more narrow economic ones, I would likely not be labeling myself "lucky" today.

My guess is that the move toward Social Security was pragmatic and not ideological. It was recognized that something had to be done about the millions of old people without means to support themselves even at the most minimal level.

A Companion Retirement System: TIAA (Teachers Insurance and Annuity Association)

While Social Security was the dominant force in creating a national movement, other retirement reforms occurred earlier. For example, I became a part of the Teachers Insurance and Annuity Association (TIAA) that was inaugurated in 1920 by philanthropists who wanted the faculty and staff in the nation's colleges and universities to retire with some dignity. This institution grew over time because its goal was so important and good. Today it is probably the largest private retirement institution in the world and remains relatively unique.

It should not be assumed that programs like TIAA and Social Security took off immediately. They did not. One problem was that they constituted significant costs for employers. The general idea was that financing retirement was a joint responsibility of employer and employee. Thus retirement meant a major new cost center for businesses. Social Security started out with a program solely for employees of business, not those in government or in the not-for-profits, like the universities. Even owners of small businesses were not included. As it became increasingly evident that providing for retirement was sensible social policy, programs expanded. Today Social Security includes about every working person.

My own experience may provide some instruction on how providing for retirement took hold and expanded. When I joined the faculty at the University of Southern California in 1951, there was essentially no retirement. I was shocked to learn that the well regarded, retired chairman of the Department of Political Science received a stipend of $200 per month as a kind of retirement payment from the University. Since the University promised no financial support to its retirees, this was regarded as a gift. I did wonder how a man, with his considerable status in the university community, could maintain his living standards on an income of about half mine as a beginning professor. I never did find out. I did not know him well. He certainly must have had other income.

After I was at the University about three years, retirement options appeared. They were not, however, high on my agenda of needs. In my early 30s, I perceived retirement as far off as the moon. I don't think I really believed I would live to age 65.

I am no longer sure of the sequence in which they appeared, but the two options provided me at the University of Southern California were Social Security and TIAA. The university did not have to join either of the programs; and so it is a credit to the institution's leadership, men of my mother's generation, that they were far-sighted and socially responsible enough to put staff interests first. In the case of Social Security, we as university employees had only to vote that we wanted to join. The tally was overwhelming, and so the University bought in, agreeing to pay half the taxes to be levied. In the case of TIAA, the University elected to join and then left it to each faculty member to make a personal decision about participation. My recollection is that all the 15 or so members of the School of Public Administration faculty joined TIAA. Again, it is important to recognize that these two retirement programs constituted a substantial hit on the general budget of the University.

The TIAA involvement was significant in another way. It is and was a "portable" pension. To the extent that there were pensions at the time, most were organization-specific. You got the pension only if you stayed with an organization for an extended period of time. You had to remain with the Los Angeles Police Department for 20 years, for example, to qualify for a pension. Where retirement plans required employee contributions, such money was often lost with a person's departure from the organization.

The great thing about TIAA was that the money we contributed, as well as the payment from the university, was ours from the day it entered the system. The employer's contribution was regarded as a cost of doing business, not something that could be withdrawn if we chose not to stay. One of my friends decided to leave USC in 1966 to join the University of California. About 40 years later, he still has his TIAA pension entitlement, now worth a considerable amount of money that will probably be inherited by his children. His was a single transfer, but many other professors have moved numerous times, carrying their pensions with them.

Pensions also became an important demand of the industrial unions, autos and steel as an example, that began to achieve great power in the 1930s. The retirement arrangements which they were successful in obtaining were "defined benefit" plans. The amount of money in a retirement account had no bearing on the size of the pension. That depended entirely on years of service and rank in the organization [usually expressed in terms of salary received over a period of three to five years}.

TIAA never operated as a "defined benefit" system. It has a "defined contribution" approach according to which the size of your pension is determined by the amount of money in your individual account.

My generation has really gained from "defined benefit" programs, which provide absolute assurance as to the amount of retirement income you will receive. This attractive feature of stability is now being lost as the defined benefit programs are being phased out.

Even the baby boomers are being impacted by this change. Businesses are free to change to "defined contribution" programs and have done so while others have simply dropped out. Thus retirement benefits, if available at all, are becoming less predictable. If the stock market goes up, as it did in 1990s, you are better off in a "defined contribution" system. If it goes down, as it generally did in 2000-2003, your assets decline. I suspect many would like to have a little of both, and that is what we have been able to get in TIAA. I have a part of my money invested in the original annuity part, which places money almost entirely in real estate mortgages. There has been a little fluctuation in these interest rates, but the return is quite stable, as in "defined benefit" programs. There is another part of the TIAA money that is invested in more speculative undertakings, essentially domestic and foreign stock funds, and thus the annuity income from this source is far more changeable.

While there are marked differences between the two approaches, it is the organization that administers your retirement money that makes a big difference. TIAA is a *nonpareil*. I don't have the least bit of insecurity that I will be fairly treated. But many employees in other organizaitons, as those in Enron, have lost essentially all their retirement savings. That's because the company administered the retirement program and counseled its people to remain heavily invested in Enron. Other companies have been as irresponsible, with increasing numbers turning bankrupt retirement systems over to the government, generally resulting in smaller pensions than promised. There are also problems with systems where employees have great discretion over their funds. They simply don't manage their money well, usually because of inattention or excessive caution.

It is hard to describe the satisfaction that comes from being an old person with adequate resources. My generation experienced a war in which most young males participated. The time spent in the military had very little economic significance for us. After our service we, as in preceding and succeeding generations, spent the better part of our lives involved in work and supporting a family. Theoretically, we had to make enough money to provide for current needs and also retirement. It was not all that easy for people on low incomes, as was the case for many, and with substantial family obligations. Social Security has been the lifesaver. As already noted, for about half of the retirees, Social Security constitutes two-thirds of their income. They obviously do not have other pensions nor have they been able to accumulate assets that provide more income. About half our retired population is placing about twice as much reliance on Social Security as the system contemplates they should. This is particularly depressing, given that these have been the best of times, living with better arrangements for retirement than were ever before available.

It is the security and independence that money brings which is really important. I cannot erase from my mind the image of very poor old people, either living unhappily with their children or persisting in disheveled and "out in the country" housing. Even at my advanced age, I do not want to be diminished as a person—and I have not been. I have a standard of life that is essentially the same as it was when I was working. Of course, the amount of money required to maintain this level is much less because I have fewer family obligations, no debt, and a small number of consumer wants. Our car, for example, is over 10 years old.

You might expect that I will next be writing that I planned and rigorously saved for this highly satisfactory outcome. Sorry to disappoint. I did not. You read regularly how people learn, often to their disappointment, how distant they are from the financial levels they need to have a satisfactory quality of life in retirement. I don't believe that Susie and I ever sat down and discussed the amount of money we needed for retirement. And that wasn't because we did not think about our finances. The difference was that we could do our retirement planning in terms of the pensions I expected to receive. I believed that my pensions would be sufficient to handle our retirement, and I was right. Personally, I think that is the way things ought to be. As we are paid in our productive years, a certain amount should be regarded as deferred income, specifically to keep us alive and well when we no longer report to work every day.

That is the way the system essentially worked for me, thanks to those grand people of a previous generation. Except for one, I was in retirement systems that regularly withdrew money that enabled me to feel secure and independent when I was too old to work. Social Security is a prime example. Throughout most of my working life, I contributed enough, along with my employer, to insure that the system was fully solvent. Indeed, the Federal government has used the surplus [backed by IOU's] to keep taxes lower than they should be. That happy situation, unfortunately, is going to come to an end in the next decade when the baby boomers retire. We need more than 2.5 workers paying into the kitty to fund our generous but really necessary benefits.

Because TIAA is actuarially sound, it is able to pay all its obligations to people like me. Contributions from employees and employers [who ought to regard their payments as deferred compensation] make it possible. The Federal system of which I am a part [things have changed a great deal since I retired] is not actuarially sound. But the Feds are incurring so much debt that an actuarially sound retirement program for employees is a small part of a much larger dilemma. The Florida state system is actuarially solid, but I can remember a time in the 1980's when Florida State University was paying 17% of my salary to bring it to that point. The system, which is "defined benefit," like the Federal, is different in that it is non-contributory. Personally, I think that is a dumb idea. Pension benefits are reduced because there is no employee contribution. Personally, I think everyone would be better off making payments and getting a greater pension benefit.

As you may have already inferred, I receive four pensions. Only in the case of Social Security do I get anything like a full pension. I moved around more than most and thus obtain my deferred compensation from several sources. There is another interesting piece of this puzzle. When you are in several systems, as I have been, you find there is a certain amount of overlapping. The only time I did not pay into Social Security, for example, was when I was in the Federal government. My contributions to TIAA began early in my career at the University of Southern California. While the contributions halted when I left the University, I began them again at Florida State University as part of a supplemental retirement program. Further, my accumulations continued to grow because of interest and stock appreciation. Partly because of the very good stock markets in the late 1980's and 1990's, TIAA produces the largest share of my retirement income today. About 40% comes from TIAA, 30% from the Federal and Florida State systems, and 30% from Social Security. This benefits profile accords with the theory that about a third of retirement income should come from Social Security.

Medicare: A More Recent and Significant Piece of the Retirement Picture

Twenty-five years ago, it never occurred to me that health costs would be a major factor in the economics of my retirement. How times change! We all know what has happened, and there is no point in rehearsing the details of this thoroughly unwelcome change in living costs.

I sometimes reflect on my attitude in 1979 when I first became a member of the Government Employees Hospital Association [now simply known as GEHA]. I got into it because it was a little cheaper than Blue Cross and because it offered a reimbursed physical examination once a year. That was a rare benefit 25 years ago. While I wanted some form of health coverage at the time, it was no big deal. Susie and I were both healthy. The kids had graduated from college and were more or less on their own. Further, the coverage was cheap, about $30 a month as I recall.

Medicare had come into being about 14 years earlier, but I did not see it as a part of my future. How wrong I was! It is 20 years that I have been covered by Medicare, and I regard it as an absolutely marvelous benefit. That is in spite of the fact that neither Susie nor I had great need for its coverage until 2004. We were the kinds of people Medicare needed to compensate for the old people with severe problems who were accounting for about 80% of its outlays. We were fortunate, too, in that GEHA developed an integrated approach that linked its benefits to those of Medicare. The monthly fee, amounting to about $225 in 2004, covers nearly all our medical costs, with the exception of half the cost of our prescription drugs.

Though I understand that universal medical coverage would be extremely costly, those over 65 can certainly appreciate its virtues. Even among the die-hard conservatives, I suspect there are few who would advocate shutting down Medicare. With aging comes the almost certain possibility of a severe illness. The security that comes from feeling the contingencies are covered [plus the fact that they are], makes life a lot easier. Most older people have fixed incomes. A big medical bill can have a very unhappy consequence for people in such financial circumstances. Susie and I learned in 2004 how Medicare works when the big bill appears. She had to have a major pancreatic operation, with overall costs of more than $30,000 at Medicare reimbursement levels. If we were not in Medicare, I am sure the bill would have been more than $50,000. So Medicare not only functions as an insurer, but its scale of operation allows it to bargain much more reasonable fees from providers. We did not have to lay out a thin dime for Susie's operation and hospitalization, Medicare covered 90% of the cost and GEHA the other 10.

It seems paradoxical that only the over-65 population in the United States enjoys such remarkable benefits. You would certainly wish them for the children who should be given the opportunity to live as healthy a life as possible. And younger adults desperately need good health in order to raise their families and to perform the work that serves the society and their more particular interests. Yet about 46 million Americans, over 15% of the population, are without any kind of health care.

You wonder how it makes sense that only those over 65 are provided complete health care and the great majority of the population is not. It is a great social tragedy that this kind of care is limited to such a few.

Medicare is the last great social reform that has touched members of my generation. This is the one great reform for which we can claim some credit. Lyndon Johnson, a generational cohort, piloted through the legislation in 1965. It was quite an accomplishment, given the fact that Harry Truman's effort to introduce universal health coverage some 15 years earlier had been badly defeated. One has to assume that the reason for the concentration on the people over 65 was that they were the sickest and most needed the help. A different argument could be made with respect to other parts of the population, but the fact is that everyone deserves adequate medical service. While my generation made at least a start in dealing with one of the most fundamental problems in modern society, it should be criticized for not doing more. It remained for the baby boomers, early in the Clinton administration, at least to make an inept stab at the problem.

Conclusion

In beginning this essay, my lone goal was to examine the assumption that the 16 million mostly young people who populated the military during World War II have a reasonable claim to being recognized as the "greatest generation." I must admit to a bias that the idea never made sense to me. When the recognition broadened to include the economic progress of the post-war world, I became even more skeptical of the validity of the claim.

While I think I have satisfied myself that we were not nearly as responsible for the winning of the war or the prosperity/affluence [much of it focused on a relatively small part of the population], I found myself coming to a much more consequential conclusion. That came about as I examined my own experience and sought to identify those elements in my environment that really made a difference in the way in which I lived. In that I used my mother as a point of comparison. I knew her to be equally as smart, as industrious, and as responsible as I or the people around me. Yet she lived a far different, much less satisfying life. My sense was that the answer did not lie in differences among generations of people but in the social and economic construction of the world around them. My situation was far different from my mother's, and it all benefitted my side of the ledger.

What accounted for these differences? Government. Pure and simple. It was massive government spending during World War II that put our factories back to work and re-established our national morale. While I am not willing to argue that war is good, it does happen that the involvement in World War II produced many advantages, primarily in reinvigorating ourselves. World War II provided employment for huge numbers of young people entering the labor market. I wonder what would have happened had there been a continuation of the situation in 1938.

In writing this, it is important to remember that these were positive events for the collectivity, not for all individuals. Far too many people died in the destructiveness of war.

In the more positive sense, the government policy that most influenced my post-war life was the GI Bill of Rights. It enabled me to secure a doctorate and to move into a thoroughly satisfying career in higher education. The Bill, passed by the Congress in 1944, did a tremendous amount to strengthen the human resources of the nation, a stimulus that I think persists to this day. It is important to realize that these fruitful and altogether generous arrangements for my generation did not involve our participation. They were provided by people much older, dating at least back to my mother's generation.

Although the education provisions of the GI Bill were far more consequential, the stimulus for housing ownership was also great. That followed a reform in the conditions of housing ownership that dated back to the earliest days of the Roosevelt administration. Today nearly 70% of the homes in the U.S. are owned by their occupants, a really significant accomplishment. Now homes are regarded as a major economic investment, not just a shelter. My generation has benefitted greatly from all these government-induced changes, further advanced by a large population increase that has made real estate costlier because of the demand.

While earlier governments set the essential terms for my life, it has also to be said that at least the first two decades after the War put us in the driver's seat. We were by far the richest country in the world, not because my generation made that happen but because we inherited it. It was unique world circumstance, one from which Americans greatly benefitted.

In retirement, there has been a reliance on two government programs, both of which have made a world of difference. One is Social Security, which was established in 1935, as part of a much larger effort to meet the needs of all Americans. It is now regarded as the "third rail of politics," because it is so popular. It is curious, and indeed gratifying, that Americans of all ages have supported the program. That may change, of course, as benefits in the future become less certain. The other program is Medicare, established in 1965 by members of my generation. It is a great program for those over 65, one that has worked and has caused me to believe totally in universal health care. It is sad that nothing of consequence in health coverage has occurred since the Medicare legislation.

The best way to judge a generation's performance is to examine what it leaves to the next generation. On this standard, I think we have been far from successful. When the hippies of the mid-sixties and early seventies declared that no one over 30 was to be trusted, they may have been right. Certainly they did not regard my generation, all of whose members were over 30, as the "greatest." Whether they were correct or not, I have a very definite opinion on how things have worked out, as of 2006. Not good.

I can list many reasons for my feelings, but I run the risk of sounding like an old codger who pines for the "good old days." Yet I do feel the need to identify some of the more obvious problems we have left to others.

Our tremendous manufacturing capacity, which set us apart from everyone else till about 1965, is long gone. Much has disappeared in the name of globalization and comparative advantage. Our trade deficit, which has been surging for decades, indicates a commitment to spend beyond our needs. We exacerbate our deficit problems by refusing to buy U.S.-made goods that carry higher price tags, which reflect reasonable compensation—current and deferred—for our people. Instead, we buy from China. I am told that not a single tennis racket is made in the U.S., though we continue to be the largest market for them. China has taken over most of their manufacture. Within these terms, it is hard to see how Americans will continue to enjoy the security and abundance that was experienced throughout the last half of the 20th century.

It goes without saying that this chronic borrowing will eventually have its effect on our position in the world. It has been written that we are the first world power that got there by going into debt. While we are clearly dominant militarily, we retain that status by running a huge domestic deficit, half a trillion a year last count. We can't afford worthy domestic programs, including universal health care, largely because we spend so much on armed might. It seems these constitute policy choices for which my generation was basically responsible.

Though it is apparent that most Americans continue to have a high standard of living, a significant change has occurred in the last three decades. We have moved from one-earner to two-earner families. To have everything a modern family seems to need, both the husband and wife have to work. However we may regard this development socially, it is obvious that many more hours are devoted to paid work than was the case in the early post-war years.

Housing is a big factor in prompting the emergence of two-earner families. Since the 1970's, real estate has been on an upward surge. The percentage of income devoted to shelter has skyrocketed in the past decades. It is anybody's guess what home ownership levels would have been had wives stayed home.

There is, of course, nothing like the comprehensive education benefits enjoyed by my generation after World War II. If we look on the GI Bill as compensation for wartime service, perhaps there should not be. Relatively few now serve in the military. If we consider the GI Bill as a major social investment, the need is always there. The education plant has, of course, grown immensely in the last half-century. The quantity data are therefore favorable. Quality is another matter. My feeling as a long-time university professor is that there has been a perceptible decline in quality. The academic calendar has been cut by a month from nine to eight months, with hours in class truncated even more. Further, standards have been lowered, with consequent grade escalation. I knew a number of students who were working full-time and also taking full loads in the university. That is certainly not the way to insure quality. With rising tuitions in public as well as private institutions, money becomes a big factor in determining the amount of time spent on academic pursuits.

Retirement poses new problems, even for our children, the baby boomers. Both Social Security and Medicare are faced with daunting financial problems in the years ahead. The retirement of baby boomers, beginning in 2008, is the critical core of the looming problem. What is unsettling is that we have known about this issue for years; and nothing has been done about it. What generation to blame?

Few, if any, steps have been taken to deal with another problem besetting Social Security: early retirement. Though our longevity has increased significantly [in 2002, 78 for a male and 82 for a woman], there has been a shocking increase in the number of people opting for reduced Social Security benefits at age 62, which are cut by 20%. In 1960 only 10% of retirees took this option; in 2002, 56% did. A friend, who took the early option, determined that he would have to reach age 78 before it would have been beneficial to wait until he was 65. Obviously, something has to give. The answer is not to water down benefits so that they do little to provide independence and security for the elderly.

As if the Social Security system were not sufficiently troublesome, private retirement systems are in worse shape, as I reported earlier. We have all but given up on "defined benefit" systems. The "defined contribution" systems are focused entirely on the individual and have their place, but they do not reflect a community/organization experience, as "defined benefit" systems do.

The health care situation seems to be even worse. "Retiree health care coverage is kind of a slowly vanishing species," the President of the Kaiser Family Foundation is reported to have said. It has also been disclosed that many companies are dropping their promises of health benefits for future retirees; and those who retired in 2004 paid premiums 25% higher than those who ended their work in 2003.

There are immense policy questions that went unanswered in my generation and continue to be ignored today, but we also have to recognize that any policy has to be implemented. Social Security worked in much of its history because it had a high quality, dedicated career staff. I am not sure that is true today. My view is that nearly all American governments are less able to perform because they have sacrificed their career systems to politics. We now think it is crucial to have people in all the leverage positions with the right ideology, rather than people with experience, knowledge and commitment to public service. The process has been going on for decades, regardless of party, and we have come to the point that the Florida governor has said it would please him greatly to see all the government buildings empty, which is the logical conclusion to Ronald Reagan's frequent assertion that government "is the enemy."

Retiring Senator Fritz Hollings of South Carolina, 83, drew the distinction between the generation that adopted Social Security and the GI Bill and the present in simple but dramatic ways. He had a goodbye interview with Mike Wallace on "60 minutes" on December 12, 2004.

He was asked by Wallace whether he felt that all those who voted Republican were racists. He replied:

"Not quite. They are conservative. They honestly don't believe in government, like we do in the Democratic party.

"We believe in feeding the hungry, and housing the homeless, and educating the uninformed and everything else like that. They believe in private education, a privatized Social Security, privatized energy policy—privatize, privatize. They don't believe in 'We the People' in order to form a more perfect union."

INDEX, VOLUME 2

Agnew Hospital, San Diego
    Nurses' Training, 24, 40-42
Albany, New York, 21, 45-46
Albany High School, 2
Aseltine, John, 62
Balch, David, 12-13, 14-15
Banco, Virginia, 119
Benbrook, Norma, 97-99
Bent, L.N., 10, 18-19
Brooklyn Elementary School, San Diego, 47, 57-58, 128
Brunswick, Georgia, 2, 10, 18-22, 43, 56, 126
Burditt, Mary, 26
California Newspaper Publishers Association, 102
Calumet, Michigan, 28-29, 33-34, 36
Carruth, Frank, 1-6, 8, 10, 16, 18
Carter, Dr. Ross, 50, 56, 65
Chamot, E.N., 5-6, 9-10
Charlottesville, Virginia, 22, 55, 121-122, 139
Chemistry, 1, 4-8, 18, 20, 23
Chula Vista, California, 15
Cincinnati, Ohio, 8, 10
Cohoes, New York, 1
Colbert, Leah, 34, 61
Colby College, 118, 121-122, 124, 130
Columbia University, 66
Columbia Scholastic Press Association, 66
Cornell University, 1, 5-7
Coronado, California, 13-14
Corsicana, Texas, 80-81, 84, 90, 126

Crandall, W.L., 14-15
Crocker, Ollie, 82-85
Dartmouth College, 67-69
    Class of 1926 Fellowship, 69
Duluth, Minnesota, 22, 27-30, 33
Ensenada, Mexico, 34-36
Federal Executive Institute, 110, 121-123, 139, 154
Florence Elementary School, San Diego, 34, 61
Florida State University, 89, 123, 165
    Department of Public Administration, 123
Folsom, Wilbur, 60
Gilloon, Virginia, 98
Golden Hill, 32, 47
    Golden Hill Playground, 58-59
Great Lakes, 26
Great Depression, 33, 109, 143-145
Guile, Mary, 26
Hall, Harvey, 66-67
Hammond, Eva, 34, 36, 39
Hercules Powder Co., 8-10, 14-18, 20-21, 23-24, 41, 43, 46
Howell
    Frances (Susie), 54, 56, 61, 76-82, 87-102, 105-116, 118, 120-126, 136-138
    John Virgil, 80-81, 85, 90-91, 126
James
    Joseph R., 27-30, 33-37, 47-49
    Elizabeth (Bess), 27, 46-53, 60, 128, 131-132, 136, 173
    Joseph H., 33-35, 37-39, 47, 49

Joseph Hammond, 27, 31-32, 36-37, 49-50
Keeley Cure, 31-32, 36
Keeley, Dr. Leslie, 31
Kelp (Seaweeed), 8, 10, 12-16
Kenvil, New Jersey, 17
Los Angeles, California, 11-13, 24, 30, 47, 72, 78, 87-88, 92-93, 98, 102, 110-114, 119-120, 122, 136-138, 155 162
Ludwig, Thomas, 63-64
Lynn, Massachusetts, 25
Macy, John, 121
Magazine San Diego, 105, 108-109
Manno, Vince, 103
Mission Beach, California, 38-39
Model T Ford, 49, 93
Mother Cabrini Institution, 86, 92
New York City, 31-32, 66
North Shores Sentinel, 72, 76, 100, 102
Northey, Salome, 27-28, 34-38
Ocean Beach, California, 38-39
    Wonderland, 38-39
    Ocean Theater, 39-40
Ogdensburg, New York, 26-27
Pacific Beach, California, 54, 72-73, 77-78, 87-88, 96-97, 100, 105, 129-130, 136-137
Pancreatic Cancer, 44
Parker, Ida, 61
Pearson, John, 24-25
Persons
    Mildred Kirk, 22-24, 55, 126-139
    Joseph Kirk, 22, 25, 27
    Elizabeth(Lois), 45, 49, 135
    Nathan, 25-26
    Edward Nathan, 26
    George Ransom, 25-26
Philadelphia, Pennsylvania, 8-10, 19
Red Jacket, Minnesota, 27-29
Resin, 18-19

Robinson
    Verna, 80-96, 98-100, 124, 126
    Joseph Simpson, 82-84
    Dovie (Julia Ann), 82-84
    Eddie, 82-84
    Mae (Aunt Bill), 83-87, 92, 98
    Della, 82-84
Rood, N.P., 19
Roosevelt Junior High School, San Diego, 34, 59, 64, 95
Rose, Henrietta, 96
Sallee, George, 80, 86
Salt Lake City, Utah, 33
San Diego, California, 8-10, 13-16, 22-24, 30-32, 34-38, 40, 42, 46-47, 50, 56-59, 61-63, 66, 69-70, 72, 78, 87-88, 90, 92-94, 100, 103-106, 108-110, 112, 128, 130, 134-135, 137, 143, 148, 157
San Diego Sun, 65-66, 145
San Diego State College, 65, 69, 100
San Diego High School, San Diego, 35, 40, 58, 61-63, 80, 96, 98
    Gray Castle, 61, 96
    The Russ, 62-64, 66
Self, Edwin, 58, 60, 64, 66-68, 72, 88, 100, 102, 136, 142, 146
Self, Dorothy McCloskey, 64
Seward, Jae, 124-126
Sharman, Maeve, 98
Sherwood
    Frank R.[8], 1, 45, 65, 132
    Clarence[9], 1-10, 16-21, 23-24, 41-46, 56, 127
    Frank P.[10], 1, 21, 23, 27, 32-34, 37-39, 41-49, 51-70, 72, 76, 78-82, 88-89, 95, 98, 100-105, 108-111, 119-127, 132-133
    Jeffrey[11] Kirk, 55, 111-119, 126
    Robin[11] Ann, 55, 111-119, 126

Evan[12], 124, 126
Lindsay[12], 89, 124, 126
Amanda[12], 124, 126
Catherine Ann, 45
Smurthwaite, Verl Freyburger, 62-63, 66
Tallahassee, Florida, 89, 124
Talley, Herbert, 15-16
Tennis, 3-5, 8, 58, 60, 124, 132, 169
Track, 3-5, 98, 129, 155
Tyler, Fred, 87-88, 93-96, 99-100
U.S. Army, 70
U.S. Department of Agriculture, 8, 13
U.S. Public Health Service, 8
   U.S. Bureau of Chemistry, 8
University of Virginia, 117, 120-121
University of California, Berkeley, 67, 88, 98-100
   Institute of Public Administration, 99
University of Southern California, 55, 59, 110, 137, 147, 155, 161-162, 165
   School of Public Administration, 119-122, 155, 162
University of California at Los Angeles, 98, 110, 137
Ventura, California, 86-87, 91-93
Washington, D.C., 51, 66, 69, 124, 126
Washington Public Affairs Center, 122
Weiss, Ruth, 98
Wesleyan University, 2-5
   Olla Podrida, 3-5
Wilmington, Delaware, 17, 20-21, 43, 124, 133
Ziolkowski
   Andrew Mark, 125-126
   Emily Ann, 89, 125-126
   Sonya Sherwood, 125-126

978-0-595-67765-8
0-595-67765-7

CPSIA information can be obtained
at www.ICGtesting.com
Printed in the USA
LVOW12*1002200316
479955LV00014B/270/P

9 780595 677658